# TEACHING
# OTHERS
# TO DEFEND
# CHRISTIANITY

# TEACHING OTHERS TO DEFEND CHRISTIANITY

## What Every Christian Should Know

# CATHRYN S. BUSE

CROSSLINK
PUBLISHING

Teaching Others to Defend Christianity

ᐁ CrossLink Publishing
ᐸ www.crosslinkpublishing.com

ISBN 978-1-63357-050-4
Library of Congress Control Number: 2015952257

# DEDICATION

To my dad—Thank you for everything.
I could not have done this without you. Love, PBD

# CONTENTS

# PREFACE

It was 1990 and I was in the fifth grade in Birmingham, Alabama. My homework assignment was to draw a picture of the Big Bang. Of course, my parents were irate that the teacher would ask the class to do such a thing. After all, we believed the Bible to be true and therefore didn't believe in the Big Bang. Instead of sending a note to the teacher attached to my completed homework assignment with his displeasure, my dad had me do a different assignment altogether. I would not be drawing the Big Bang; instead, I would be drawing a picture of the earth with the verse Genesis 1:1 neatly written as its caption. But this would not be done on the required notebook page size. No, my picture would be done on a poster board so that it could not be dismissed by the teacher and quietly slid into the stack of papers of other homework assignments. I was mortified at the suggestion. But at that moment, I understood the stand my dad wanted me to take. It was in this moment that he set the tone for what would be a lifetime of upholding the truth of the Bible in the face of the secularism taught in school—even deep within the Bible belt.

After high school, I attended the University of Alabama in Huntsville where I graduated summa cum laude with a Bachelor of Science in Engineering and a Master of Science in

Engineering. I worked for nearly ten years in the engineering field supporting Department of Defense missile programs, commercial rocket manufacturing, and NASA design programs. From my experience in the technical arena with both my education and career, I continually witnessed the deep-rooted skepticism in our society of the claims made by religion in general and the Bible in particular. I found that people had more challenging questions for Christianity than just if Jesus loves them. The people I encountered were asking whether God existed at all, if the Bible could be trusted, if there were an afterlife, and whether there were multiple ways to that afterlife.

Despite the fact I had attended a solid, Bible-teaching church since my childhood, the foundational truths that address those concerns were never taught. The church had not prepared me to answer the types of questions the critical-thinking community had. As an engineer advocating for the case of Jesus, I saw how desperately the church needed to be teaching apologetics; yet, it was not. For years my parents and others like them sent their children to church expecting the church to prepare us for the battles against the world. But instead, we had been given superficial Christian platitudes with no depth or foundation. Many of my peers stumbled in their faith when faced with the questions the world threw at them in college. While I clung to my faith as truth, I knew I needed to understand why it was truth.

It was from that desire to give my classmates and coworkers the answers they so desperately needed that I began studying apologetics. I continued researching the topic for over fifteen years. It became my passion to find those answers not just to solidify my own faith but to help others see that there is reason and truth behind the Christian faith. Seeing the struggles of my friends encouraged me to pursue a way to bring thinking minds into faith in Jesus, to merge the intellectual with the spiritual. While I do not have a theological degree, I have found that for some critical-thinking minds, a masters in engineering can gain more respect and trust for a theological discussion than a religious doctorate. It can show them that the foundational truths of Christianity are not just logical to those educated within the church, but to those technically-minded people educated outside the church as well.

The church can no longer neglect its responsibility to prepare the believer to navigate through all the competing ideas and philosophies the world offers. Schools, media, and society are peddling the idea that science trumps religion, that the Bible is out of date, and that all religions are equal. The church must begin educating and preparing its congregation to counter that kind of ideology. My passion for apologetics led me to do just that. I started teaching this material to high school students at my church so that they would be better prepared to face the world's questions. Those classes grew to include adult classes across the community, across denominations, and across cities because these truths apply to anyone who calls on the name of Jesus as their Lord and Savior. *Teaching Others to Defend Christianity* is the result of that effort to educate others on those foundational truths to Christianity, whether it's gaining confidence that God does exist, that Biblical creation is true, or that God is in control even in our suffering. It has been used to reach people of all ages and backgrounds—from twelve-year olds to eighty-five-year olds, from high school students to stay-at-home mothers, from college students to adults in retirement. It is my desire that people everywhere are able to take these foundational truths and teach them to other believers and to unbelievers so that we can all increase in our confidence and faith in Jesus Christ. *Teaching Others to Defend Christianity* gives the teacher the confidence and tools necessary to accomplish that.

When Luke set out to write his Gospel, he stated his purpose was so that Theophilus "may know the certainty of those things" in which he was instructed. If you are a Christian and know that

Jesus Christ is your Savior, my desire is that this book will solidify your faith, confirming the certainty of those things in which you have been instructed. I pray that it will give you the confidence and the preparation to go into the unsaved world and share with others the reason for the hope that lies within you. If you do not know Christ as your Savior, I hope that you would read this book with an open mind and heart truly seeking the truth. I pray that the Lord would impress on you the certainty of His presence, His greatness, His love, and His mercy that He has offered to all mankind. He chose to give of Himself and step out of the throne room of heaven for the express purpose of suffering and dying for us while we were still sinners. He who knew no sin became sin for us so that we could have His righteousness, the righteousness which is required by our Creator to come into His presence.

My goal is to glorify our great God and Father and to announce the wondrous gift of salvation to as many as will hear and respond to His calling. This is my goal and the goal of every Christian, and it should be the goal of every person teaching this material. To His glory forever and ever. Amen.

# HOW TO USE THIS BOOK

*Teaching Others to Defend Christianity* is for anyone who wants to deepen and strengthen their Biblical foundations of faith wherever they may be in their life. It is to help the Christian understand why they should believe Christianity is truth and to prepare the believer to be a more effective witness to the world. While anyone can use this as a resource in their own walk, *Teaching Others to Defend Christianity* has been specifically designed as a teaching tool. The teacher can teach directly from this material to logically walk the class from an atheistic worldview, to evidence that there is a god, to the uniqueness of the Christian God, to the validity of the New Testament, and finally to the certainty that Jesus is the Son of God.

*Teaching Others to Defend Christianity* is structured so that each chapter is a one-hour class session. The six chapters are to be taught in sequential fashion to build the case in a progression from atheism to belief in Jesus Christ. Each chapter begins with an introduction to review what has been covered in the previous lessons, followed by a study section that has the current lesson material. The end of each chapter has a list of questions for further consideration. These can be used during the session for additional group discussion, or for the student to consider on their own as they review the material. Supplemental slideshow material is also available on the CrossLink website to assist in presenting each lesson: www.crosslinkpublishing.com/shop/teaching-others-to-defend-christianity/ Additional information can also be found on the Defend the Faith Ministry site at www.defendthefaithministry.com

For the student, this study is a thought-provoking and an intense look at the evidences that affirm to us that our belief is not placed in "invented stories" but is standing on the solid ground of truth. It is not to be taken lightly and it is not for those who desire a surface-level explanation of Biblical truths. This book touches on the laws of thermodynamics, DNA replication, physics, philosophical reasoning, and archeology. It is for those that welcome the challenge to think about what they believe so that they may be able to bring other thoughtful minds into that same belief.

For the teacher, you don't have to be an expert in science or philosophy to lead this study. This book will explain all of those points on an understandable level. However, it is necessary that you read through this material in its entirety before beginning to teach. It is important to see the case being built by each lesson so that you can impart that to the students. You must know where each chapter is heading in order to guide the class in the right direction. Remember, no one will have all the answers to every question asked. The best approach is to be honest when you are not sure and to assure the student that you will research the topic to provide an answer at a later time. Be confident, though, because we have truth on our side!

There is a hunger out there for a more intellectual and deeper understanding of the Christian faith. *Teaching Others to Defend Christianity* provides those fundamental apologetics truths in an applicable way. This study is a stimulating and challenging study to answer the most important question posed to mankind: "What shall I do with this Jesus who is called the Christ?" I applaud you for taking on this important task to teach people how to defend their faith and to have confidence that there is a God and that Jesus Christ is Lord.

# INTRODUCTION

Does God exist? Aren't all religions the same? Isn't the Bible just a bunch of stories changed over generations? Wasn't Jesus just a good man? Can't we believe anything as long as we're sincere? These are becoming increasingly common questions that the world around us has for Christianity. The skepticism of our society does not accept "because the Bible says so" as an answer. Unfortunately, many churches do not adequately equip its members to answer these questions. That does a disservice to Christians desiring to grow in their faith and to the world around us when we fail to give a logical reason for the hope that lies within us. We have to be able to explain to the world why God is real and Jesus is the truth. Furthermore, it is so important that we know how to address those questions because it solidifies our own faith and gives us confidence in what we believe. If we aren't fully grounded in the truth of what we believe, then we too can be swayed away from it by those who challenge it.

*Teaching Others to Defend Christianity* addresses each of those questions by taking the reader through a logical progression from questioning God's existence to finding salvation through Jesus. It will methodically move the reader from no God, to establishing that there is a God, that it is the Christian God, and that we have certainty in the claims made by Jesus Christ as the Son of God. The first three lessons provide several arguments using multiple fields of science and philosophy to establish that a god must exist. Through cosmology, biology, astronomy, physics, philosophy, and anthropology, there is evidence that a god exists to account for our design, our existence, and our morality. Once the existence of a god has been established, then it must be determined which god created us and which god is worthy of our worship.

By comparing the doctrines of several major world religions, it is evident that the Christian God is unique. Only the Christian God provides a way to solve the issue of our sin through Jesus. Jesus claimed to be the way, the truth, and the life, and that no one comes to the Father except through Him. Because Christianity is therefore inseparable from the divinity of Jesus as the Son of God, we must assess the validity of His claim. In that endeavor, the authenticity and credibility of the New Testament accounts of His life must first be established. Once it is proven that the New Testament is trustworthy, a logical assessment must be made of the claims in the New Testament about the life, death, and resurrection of Jesus. Considering the evidence of God's existence, the uniqueness of the Christian God, and the proof of the deity and resurrection of Jesus, there is no other logical conclusion to reach than that Jesus Christ was who He claimed to be as the Son of God. Only through Him can the world be reconciled to God.

# DOES GOD EXIST?

Psalm 14:1 The fool has said in his heart, "There is no God."

# LESSON 1

## The Cosmological Argument

### INTRODUCTION

This study is a six-week investigation into the foundational truths of Christianity. It will logically progress from atheism (there is no God) to belief in Jesus Christ (the Son of God). It seems difficult for an atheist to understand why they need to believe in Jesus for reconciliation to God if they don't believe there is a God at all. So we will spend the first three weeks looking at different ways to be confident that a God does exist. After establishing that a God must exist, we have to determine which God it is. We will show the unique solution provided by the Christian God that sets Him apart from all other world religions. That solution comes to us through the life, death, and resurrection of Jesus Christ. So we will then confirm the authenticity of the accounts of His life found in the New Testament. Lastly, we will investigate the impact of those claims found in the New Testament and assess their validity. The overarching idea is to show how we can move from the idea that there is no God to faith in Jesus without having to remove our intellect from the process. The belief of Jesus is not built on invented stories but on the solid foundation of truth in every way that it is studied.

## STUDY

Does God exist? Either He does or He doesn't; there is no in-between.

It is reasonable to suggest that if there is a God, then He would have left us enough evidence to determine that He does exist. But God still has to allow us to make a choice about Him, to exercise faith. If God gave us absolute proof that He existed, then you could not deny Him anymore than you can deny the sun in the sky. Therefore, you couldn't choose to believe in Him anymore than you choose the sunrise to start the day. But if He gave us no proof, then we could never get to a point to find Him. Consequently, He has to leave us just enough evidence so that those who want to find Him can.[1]

The proof of God's existence that many people demand to see is oftentimes in a physical sense of proof. *How can we say God exists if we can't physically touch him, feel him, or see him?* Not everything that we are sure exists can be proven through those types of physical measures. Things like love, intelligence, sadness, air, or gravity can't be seen directly yet they are very real things. The evidence we have for the existence of those things is found in other ways: love can be demonstrated; gravity can be experienced; intelligence can be presumed; sadness can be felt. There are cumulative evidences of the effects of these things that let us know they do exist. The fact that those things are invisible does not make them any less real.

God gave us enough evidence to determine that He does exist. We can't touch God directly, so we have to prove His existence through other ways. *So what would that evidence be if we can't weigh, measure, or observe God directly?*

- o Experiential. We can experience God on a personal level. For the believer, this can be very real evidence for God's existence. Unfortunately, however, that doesn't always stand up as evidence in the mind of an unbeliever. They may feel or experience things themselves, but they choose to attribute that to something other than god. They may use the words fate or luck or even just a generic term of providence. Using experiential evidence won't even help when discussing other religions either. Muslims attribute things to Allah, Buddhists attribute things to karma, a Christian may say things are divine intervention, and an atheist would say it's a mere coincidence. How do we know which is the truth?
- o Presumption of fact. Many people demand proof of the existence of God but not everything is proven in the same way. When people make that claim they are generally expecting a proof through the scientific method but we accept many other things as proof even though they are not attained through experimentation or through sensory evidence.

We can prove something by providing enough evidence to establish the **presumption of fact.** And that fact will stand to be true based on solid presumption unless the fact can be refuted otherwise. This is what is used even in our own court of law. We cannot repeat the past so many times we rely on presumption of fact to establish what most likely occurred.

For example, you walk into a room and find a glass of water sitting on the counter. You didn't witness anyone pouring the water into the glass, but you can presume that someone did in fact pour water into the glass. There is the presumption of fact that someone poured a glass of water, and that fact will stand to be true unless someone can refute it by proving otherwise. In the same way, we have the presumption of fact that because of what we can observe in the world, there must be a god who is responsible for its existence. That fact will stand to be true unless it can be proved otherwise.

## COSMOLOGICAL ARGUMENT

The universe exists; therefore, its existence must be explained in some way. We have to answer the question, *"Why is there something rather than nothing?"*[2] This is defined by the relationship between cause and effect. And there are several laws, known as the laws of causality, which explain this relationship.[3]

1. Every material effect (or anything that exists that had a beginning) must have a cause. You **cannot have an effect without a cause;** you cannot have a cause without an effect. In other words, an effect must have a cause or else it ceases to be an effect. Likewise, a cause must have an effect or else it ceases to be a cause.

   For example, if water is poured into a glass, then it will be full of water. The cause is the pouring of water. The effect is the glass has water in it. The glass could not have water in it (effect) without someone pouring it in (cause). And you can't have someone pour water into the glass (cause) without water being in it (effect).

2. The **effect must always follow the cause.** The cause will never follow the effect. The glass cannot have water in it, and then water was poured in.

3. The effect is always an **adequate effect** related to the cause. The effect and cause must be adequate to one another. So if we observe an effect, there must be an adequate cause.

    Water being poured into a glass (cause) did not result in a river flooding (effect). That effect is not adequate to the cause.

If the universe (a material entity) exists, something must have caused it. The universe is the effect, so *what was the cause*? There are only three possible options for this:[4]

1. The universe is eternal. The universe has always existed and will always continue to exist. An eternal universe would not need a cause because there was never a time when there wasn't a universe.

If the universe is not eternal, then there are two possible explanations within that.

2. The universe is not eternal and it created itself.
3. The universe is not eternal and it did not create itself.

*Option 1: The Universe Is Eternal*

In the 1920s, scientists relied on the argument that the universe was eternal to avoid having to account for a god. If the universe were eternal, then it would have no beginning or end. There would be no need for a "first cause" of the universe. These scientists developed the Steady State theory (or infinite universe) based on the idea of continuous creation of matter in the universe.[5] If this theory were true, then there would be no need to find the cause for this effect. Only things that have a beginning need an explanation as to how they began. If something is eternal, it does not require a cause.

However, in 1915 Einstein's Theory of Relativity indicated that the universe had a starting point in time. Decades later through the Hubble Telescope, scientists observed that the universe was expanding and thus concluded the universe must have a starting point from which to expand. They even coined a term to refer to this beginning: the Big Bang Theory. It shows they discovered the universe goes back to a *singularity event* where everything started. The Big Bang Theory basically admits that the universe began at some point. At first glance it seems odd to use the Big Bang Theory in a proof about God but it does give theists an advantage. Science has proven the universe had a beginning. Therefore, something had to have caused it to begin.[6]

The idea of an eternal universe is also disproven through two laws of thermodynamics.[7]

1. The First Law of Thermodynamics states that neither matter nor energy is created or destroyed in nature. Matter can be converted to energy and energy can be converted to matter but the total of amount of matter and energy in the universe will remain constant. So we have the same amount of matter and energy now as we have always had. Following this law, it makes it impossible for the universe to create its own matter.

In other words, there couldn't have been an eternity of one atom that eventually spawned additional atoms and energy to grow into the amount of matter we see today. Matter cannot be further created so what we observe today is what we started with. It had to have been placed here by some cause.

This strikes the first blow to the Steady State theory's assumption that the universe continuously creates its own matter. This also indicates that the universe had a beginning. Some cause had to initially establish this finite amount of matter and energy because matter and energy cannot still be created within nature itself.

2. The Second Law of Thermodynamics states that all things tend towards entropy — or disorder and decay, *unless energy is applied into the system.* For an example, look at your backyard. If you leave it to itself, it will grow full of weeds unless you put energy into it, which would be you cutting the grass. This means that the Universe is running down like a clock continuing into decay and disorder. But if things are moving towards disorder, then at one point things were fully ordered. Our "clock" was fully wound up.

More importantly, it shows that the universe is not in a steady state. Something that is eternal would be in a steady state because it would not show any degeneration. Eternal things do not decay. Since our universe is degenerating, it is not eternal. It shows the universe has a beginning, and it will have an end.

**Conclusion**: the universe is NOT eternal

*Option 2: The Universe Created Itself*

If the universe is not eternal, then that means it is finite. It has a beginning, and that beginning must be explained. Going back to our possible scenarios, the first assessment of a finite universe is that it created itself. Restating that in light of our understanding of the laws of causality, this would mean that the universe would be both the cause AND the effect. *Could that be possible?*

From the earlier example of the water-filled glass, that would mean the water-filled glass caused itself to be filled with water. The effect (the glass full of water) must also be the cause (the glass full of water). It is illogical to think the cause and effect could ever be the same thing.

It also means that the universe would have to exist in order to create itself. And now we have some circular logic. *How can something create itself if it doesn't exist yet?*

> *As stated by theologian R.C. Sproul: "For something to bring itself into being it must have the power of being within itself. It must at least have enough causal power to cause its own being. If it derives its being from some other source, then it clearly would not be either self-existent or self-created. It would be, plainly and simply, an effect. Of course, the problem is complicated by the other necessity we've labored so painstakingly to establish: it would have to have the causal power of being before it was. It would have to have the power of being before it had any being with which to exercise that power."*[8]

Breaking that down, it means that first something must have the power of creation within itself. Unless something has enough power to create itself, it is only an effect and therefore requires a cause. But it is compounded by the fact that in order to create yourself, you would have to already exist to create yourself. It becomes a circular logic problem.

If an entity cannot account for its own existence, meaning it could not have caused itself, then it is dependent on something outside itself to explain its existence. This is known as contingent. The question becomes whether the universe is contingent or not. If it is contingent (dependent on something to create it), then what is it that is responsible for its existence?

**Conclusion**: the universe did not create itself

*Option 3: The Universe Was Created*

We've established that the universe has a beginning and therefore is an effect requiring an adequate cause. And we've established that the cause could not be the universe itself. That leaves us with the only logical option that the universe had to be created by something other than itself.

So what was it? We can deduce a few characteristics of that cause based on our knowledge of the laws of causality.

1. Whatever created the universe **must have existed before it**. The cause must come before the effect. The creator of the universe could not come into being AFTER the universe exists. So whatever made the universe existed before the universe in order to create it.

2. Whatever created the universe **must be superior to the universe**. The creator has to be greater than the created; the creation cannot be superior to the creator. For example, computers are only as smart as we make them.

3. Whatever created the universe **must have a different nature** than the universe.[9] Everything in this universe is finite and contingent (that is what we have just established through this analysis). Nothing that we observe here in this universe is capable of creating this universe. This finite, contingent universe of matter is unable to explain itself, so the creator of this universe must be different from what is here in the universe.

Some people may struggle with this point about creating something of a different nature by confusing the idea of creation with procreation. We, as humans, can "create" another human in our common vernacular, but that is in actuality procreation. We reproduce another human, instead of making a human *ex nihilo*, or out of nothing. A child I create is formed from preexisting DNA. The creation of the universe would have to be formed using nothing at all. It would go from nothing to then suddenly everything.

The creator of this universe must exist outside this universe. The universe by definition consists of time, space, energy, and matter. Therefore whatever caused the universe must exist outside of time, space, energy, and matter. You can call it whatever you want—aliens, Bob the Builder, or the cosmic originator—but those characteristics are what we attribute to God. Even if you don't want to call it God, the fact remains that something outside of our universe is responsible for creating this universe.

## Who Made God?

The natural progression from this point is to then question who made God. *If God made the universe, then who made God?* But, remember, only things that have a beginning require a cause to bring it into being. We haven't proven that God has a beginning (unlike our proof that the universe has a beginning). Since God is eternal, He has no beginning, and therefore does not require a cause.

*How can we assert that God is eternal?* Are we avoiding the question by making that claim? Not at all. Because we exist now, *something* had to have existed forever. Since science has proven that the universe has a beginning, then there was a time when there was **no universe**. But we know that nothing produces nothing. We can't get something from nothing.[10] If there had ever been a time when nothing existed (no universe **and** no eternal God), then there would still be nothing now.

Because something does exist now, it follows that *something* had to exist forever—and we would assign that something to be a creator, or God. R.C. Sproul states: "Indeed, reason demands that if something exists, either the world or God (or anything else), then **something** must be self-existent....**There must be a self-existent being of some sort somewhere or nothing would or could exist.**"[11]

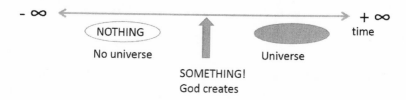

These arguments explain the existence of matter and our physical world. But we also have a world of the mind, intelligence, morality, information, and emotion. Those things can't come from nothing, just like matter can't come from nothing. Intelligence (for example our DNA code) cannot generate itself. Things of the mind, or knowledge, cannot come from nothing either. We are alive with a working mind, and we are aware of our existence. Something had to give us that awareness, something bigger than ourselves.[12]

We have those things because the cause has given those things to us. If the effect has a characteristic, it only has it because the cause has given it that characteristic. The cause cannot give to the effect what it does not have. Ergo, the effect cannot have something that the cause did not provide to it. The Bible would describe this as being "made in the image of God."

*Norman Geisler states it this way: "If my mind or ability to know is received, then there must be a Mind or Knower who gave it to me. The intellectual does not arise from the nonintellectual; something cannot arise from nothing."[13]*

To believe that intelligent and complex life was formed out of nothing, as atheists would have you believe, breaks with any scientific reasonable belief and possibility. The cause found within the atheistic explanation (which they say would be nothing) is not adequate to produce the effect of a complex and intelligent Universe.

Conclusion

How did we come to be here? Every material and mental effect must have an adequate cause that comes before it. The universe exists and its existence must be explained in some way.

From the laws of thermodynamics, the Theory of Relativity, and observations in science using the Hubble Telescope, we know that the universe is not eternal. It has a beginning and will have an end; it is an effect that requires a cause. Logically, we conclude that the universe could not have created itself. It is contingent on something else bringing it into existence. Therefore, something outside of the universe caused the universe to be.

Because we have something now, we know that something existed before us and outside of us in order to create us. The universe, intelligent life, morality, and love all exist as an effect. The effect cannot be greater than the cause or precede the cause. We must conclude that the cause of life must be a living intelligent Creator who is also loving and moral.

The cosmological argument uses logic and science to show that because we exist, something must have caused us to come into existence. This argument shows there must be an Uncaused and Eternal Cause.

**QUESTIONS FOR CONSIDERATION**

What are some things that we know are real but are not visible to us?

Why is using our personal experience of God not a convincing argument of God's existence to an unbeliever?

How is the presumption of fact used to prove the existence of God?

Why is it important to show that the universe is not eternal? How do we know that it is not?

Could the universe create itself?

Why does the creator of the universe have to have a different nature than this universe?

Why does God not need a creator?

How do we know that whatever created us must be eternal?

What is the adequate cause for the material, intelligent, loving, and moral effect that is our universe? What is the presumption of fact?

# LESSON 2

## The Teleological Argument

**INTRODUCTION**

Last lesson we discussed the cosmological argument for how we know there is a Creator. The universe exists and its existence must be explained in some way. Through the laws of thermodynamics, findings from the Hubble telescope, and Einstein's Theory of Relativity, we know scientifically that the universe is not eternal. This means that the universe has a beginning, which makes it an effect. It logically follows that the effect must have an adequate cause that came before it. The universe could not have caused itself because it is impossible for the universe to be both the cause and the effect. Therefore, the universe must have been created by something that existed before it, is superior to it, and is of a different nature. Whatever it is that created this universe exists outside of this finite universe. So the cause for the effect that is our universe must be eternal. Something must have always existed because there is something now.

The cosmological argument is one way to logically and scientifically deduce with the presumption of fact that a God must exist to cause our universe to come into being. The next argument, the teleological argument, will look at the evidence in biological design to show that we have been specifically designed for life in this universe.

## STUDY

Teleology refers to purpose or design. So the teleological argument states where there is purposeful design in a system, there must be a designer. Order, planning, and design in a system are indicative of intelligence, purpose, and specific intent as the originating cause.

> When you look at the Mona Lisa, you can infer there was in fact a painter because it has a design to it. From presumption of fact, we can presume that there must exist somewhere a painter. That is the most logical conclusion unless it can be proved otherwise.

In the 1800s this was put forth by William Paley as the "watch argument." Imagine you were walking along the street and found a watch lying on the ground. Upon close inspection of the watch and its intricate system of perfectly matched cogs and gears, you could deduce that there was a watchmaker. Paley used this argument to justify an intelligent designer for the universe. He could see the design within the universe and therefore deduced that there must have been a designer.[1]

Atheists would agree that design requires a designer, but atheists disagree that the universe has any design in it. If the universe doesn't have design, then the universe doesn't need a designer. Richard Dawkins, our time's leading evolutionist, put this argument forward as the blind watchmaker. In the foreword to his book, *The Blind Watchmaker,* Dawkins states:

> *There may be good reasons for belief in God, but the argument from design is not one of them ... despite all appearances to the contrary, there is no watchmaker in nature beyond the blind forces of physics.... Natural selection, the unconscious, automatic, blind yet essentially nonrandom process that Darwin discovered, and that we now understand to be the explanation for the existence and form of all life, has no purpose in mind. It has no mind and no mind's eye. It does not plan for the future. It has no vision, no foresight, no sight at all. If it can be said to play the role of watchmaker in nature, it is the blind watchmaker.[2]*

Dawkins believes that physics, natural selection, and mutations explain everything in the universe, and the universe does not have any design to it. The issue then becomes not whether a design has to have a designer, but whether there is design in the universe at all. So we must answer the questions: *is there design in the universe?*

Evidence of Non-design

The atheist most likely will reference examples of "non-design," those things that appear to be a poor design or seemingly useless to the organism. Many people reference our appendix as an example of non-design because it doesn't appear to serve a purpose. The atheist's argument is that if there were a God designing this world, then things would not have elements of seemingly useless, non-designed features.

However, non-designed features can sometimes be explained. Something that appears to us as non-design might not actually be non-design. It might be that at this point in time we don't see the purpose in that feature.

A good example is found in the panda's thumb, which is basically a sixth digit in the panda's palm. Dr. Jay Gould, a leading proponent of suboptimality (or the non-design argument), wrote his book, *The Panda's Thumb*, to explain that this sixth digit is utterly useless to the panda. He describes how the panda already has five other digits on its "hands," so the existence of this oddly placed pseudo-thumb cannot be explained as having any function to the panda. He even says, "Odd arrangements and funny solutions are the proof of evolution—paths that a sensible God would never tread, but that a natural process, constrained by history, follows perforce."[3]

However, since the time Dr. Gould wrote that, researchers have studied the use of the panda's thumb and have made some interesting observations. They found that by using this thumb, the panda has the ability to grip things as tightly and with as much precision as humans—and they are one of a few large animals that can do so.

*Researchers in the book* The Giant Pandas of Wolong *stated: "The panda can handle bamboo stems with great precision by holding them as if with forceps in the hairless groove connecting the pad of the first digit and pseudothumb."*[4]

Similarly, the oft-cited example of the useless appendix may be wrong as well. Recent research has discovered that the appendix actually functions like a storehouse for good bacteria. It can be tapped into as a reboot for the digestive system after suffering from cholera or dysentery.[5] This seemingly useless organ from our first-world perspective may not be so useless after all! There may be other cases then of what appears to be non-design that later are proven to be unique, intelligent design after all.

The other issue with declaring things as suboptimal in nature is it makes the assumption that one knows the absolute standard of optimal. The atheist places himself as the judge of what is considered optimal, but on what is he basing its optimality? The assessment of optimal is based on subjectivity and the supposed nature of the Creator. Those who claim that something is "suboptimal" must, by definition, set themselves up as the sole judge of what is, and what is not, optimal. The atheist must assume himself as the Creator, presuppose the mind of the Creator, and then postulate what the Creator did or did not do correctly.[6]

> Leading evolutionist Douglas Futuyma admits this presumption himself: "The case for evolution has ... evidence that the natural world does not conform to **our expectation** of what an omnipotent, omniscient, truthful Creator **would have** created (emphasis added)."[7] It means they assess creation based on how they would have created it.

There are also instances where the atheist is judging evidence of suboptimality but what he's actually observing is nature's degeneration. When sin entered the world through Adam and Eve, the world began its degenerative process. We have diseases, illnesses, and degenerative genetic mutations because of our sin nature, not because we were not created by a God.

> For example, if you were digging through your grandmother's attic and found an old book that smelled musty, and the pages were all yellowed and stuck together—would you consider the writer of the book to be unintelligent because the book is so old and musty? Would you assume that there were no author at all because it's yellowed and illegible? That would be ridiculous.

> Or, consider a machine designed to produce tin cans that begins making bent cans. Does that mean that the

machine didn't have a designer? Or is it more likely that the machine has worn down? Maybe the machinist didn't properly operate it. The fact that the **product** of an orderly mechanism is flawed does not mean there is not a designer of that mechanism. It is the **existence** of the orderly mechanism itself that demands a designer.

*So do examples of non-design indicate that there is no Designer?* Not at all! Even though there might be examples of things that are not useful in the design of an organism, the theist only needs to show that some things do have a design. You can certainly have non-design features and still have a designer, but you can't have design features and have no designer.

The existence of the appendix does not suddenly negate the existence of chemically coded information in a DNA molecule. Consider the initial example of a painting requiring a painter. Imagine a room covered with random splatters of paint on the walls but with the Mona Lisa hanging up in the corner. The random splatters of paint do not negate the existence of a painter because obviously the Mona Lisa required a painter.

Design of the Universe

Now that we have addressed the concern about evidence of non-design, let's take a look at the extensive evidence that there is design by starting with the universe itself.

Our universe is incredibly precise, something known as **anthropic fine-tuning**. The fundamental laws and parameters of physics have precise numerical values. If the universe were non-designed (and thus, random as it would be if the Big Bang Theory were true), then these laws of physics could have theoretically been any value out of infinity. Or more simply put, the values conceivably could have been anything besides what they are. There would be no reason for them to have the value that we know them to have. However, all of those laws and parameters have the exact value necessary, **individually** and **all together**, to support life in this universe.[8]

> For example, the value for Earth's gravity could have been any number out of infinity. Moving one notch on the infinite number line would be miniscule in the grand scheme of possible values. But altering its value by only one notch on that number line would have catastrophic effects on the universe. That is how precise the value for gravity must be here on earth in order to maintain life.[9]

The same level of precision can be found in the strong and weak nuclear force that holds atoms together, the expansion rate of the universe, the electromagnetic force, the cosmological constant (the energy density of empty space), and some **thirty** other separate physical or cosmological parameters that require such precise calibration in order to sustain life on our planet.[10]

It is improbable to think that each of those parameters would have accidentally and randomly been set at the precise value necessary for life. And the improbability is compounded even further when you consider that each of those parameters had to be at that precise value **all at the same time**.

> In other words, it would do us no good if all the parameters were precisely correct except for earth's gravity or except for the strong and weak nuclear force. It requires all of those to be correct together at the same time with that level of precision for life to exist.

> Consider the specifications of the Earth within the universe for life to be here.

- The Earth rotates on its axis at 1,000 miles an hour at the equator and moves around the sun at 70,000 miles an hour. As the Earth moves around the Sun, it departs from a straight line by only one-ninth of an inch every 18 miles. If it departed by one-eighth of an inch we would come so close to the Sun that we would burn up. If we departed by only one-tenth of an inch, then we would be too far from the Sun and we would all freeze. The Earth is even tilted at exactly 23.5 degrees. Any difference in that and our waters would pool at the south and north poles, leaving more desert wasteland.[11]
- If our atmosphere were any thinner, then meteorites could more easily and more forcefully strike the Earth. Our earth is even protected from meteorite strikes because of the precise size, relational location, and gravitational pull of Jupiter.[12]
- If the orbit of the earth around the sun were slowed down, our seasons would be too long and we wouldn't be able to grow any crops due to the long stretch of heat and cold. If the orbit of the earth were sped up, then the growing season wouldn't be long enough to grow crops before the cold winters. The speed of the earth's orbit and the distance of the earth from the sun are perfectly calculated to allow for seasons to maintain life.[13] Those seasons are critical for the existence of plant life, those things that just happen to "breathe in" what we breathe out (carbon dioxide) and vice versa to create the perfect balance in life.
- Even the amount of water on the Earth is critical for that perfect balance between animal and plant life. About four-fifths of the Earth is covered by oceans. Since water heats and cools at a slower rate than land, the water serves as a natural heating and cooling system for the land mass on Earth. We also depend on botany for our oxygen

supply. But approximately 90 percent of that oxygen comes from microscopic plants in the seas. If our oceans were appreciably smaller, we would soon be out of air to breathe.[14]

- Speaking of our oceans, the Earth is 240,000 miles from the moon, and its gravitational pull is responsible for our ocean tides. If the moon were closer to the Earth by only one-fifth that distance, then the tides would be so enormous twice a day that they would reach 35 to 50 feet high over most of the Earth. The moon is perfectly positioned from the earth to control the tides.[15]

The earth is perfectly placed and perfectly oriented such that there is life here. This universe is uniquely adapted to provide for life here on earth. The physical laws of nature are amazingly precise and mutually dependent on each other's precision for that life to be maintained.

Could random chance really account for such precision?

What is the logical presumption of fact for the earth to have this precise balance for life to exist? It is not statistically likely for all of those things to occur, at those **exact values**, at the **same time** by random chance. If it cannot be from random chance, **then it must be designed**.

What does this mean then that the universe's precision is such that it must have been designed? It means that this kind of orderly precision cannot arise from something chaotic. The Second Law of Thermodynamics establishes this fact. All things tend toward entropy (chaos, disorder, or decay), unless energy is applied to the system. A random chaotic event left unattended cannot become ordered and planned, unless something else enters into that system to order it. A random explosion of chaos cannot fall into an orderly design. Therefore, the Big Bang could not have resulted in this highly complex, interconnected, and perfectly symbiotic universe. This universe was designed in this fashion so that life could exist here.

The universe's precision is evidence that it is planned, ordered, and designed. From these specifications of life on earth, even Richard Dawkins admits, "The more statistically improbable a thing is, the less we can believe that it just happened by blind chance. Superficially, the obvious alternative to chance is an intelligent Designer."[16]

## Design of the Human Body

There is evidence of design on the large scale of the universe, but let's investigate if there is evidence of design on the smallest scale within the basic building block of all life, the cell.

### Design in the Cell

The human body can be broken down into four major levels: systems (reproductive, circulatory, muscular, etc.); organs (heart, liver, kidney, etc.); tissues (muscle tissue, nervous tissue, etc.); and cells. The cell represents the smallest unit of life and is amazingly complex. All living organisms are comprised of these cells which are just arranged in different ways to generate all the variety of life.

But is the cell's complexity a result of random mutation on something simple, or does it show evidence of design? This is the question that must be continually revisited.

*If something complex could not have been assembled by randomly building up on something simple, then it **must have been designed**. For each observation made in biology, this question must be posited, and it must be honestly answered without bias: Is it more logical that these complicated biological* mechanisms arose from random disorder or from an organized designer? *What is the presumption of fact here?*

Cells have three major components:

The first component is the **cell membrane** and is what encloses the entire cell. It is responsible for keeping all the cell's components together and for protecting the cell from external environments. That seems like a very straightforward task; however, the cell does need some things to be able to enter and exit. The cell membrane must selectively determine from the hundreds of compounds around it what things can enter the cell safely and what things should exit the cell based on the cell's requirements. Yet how does the cell know what those requirements are? The cell must somehow know what things are safe to enter and what things are necessary to exit. If it gets that basic analysis wrong, then the life of the cell would be compromised. And the cell does not have generations to try to get this right. If the cell dies in the first generation, then there is no cell to try again the next generation.

The second major component is the **cytoplasm**. It is a watery matrix that holds all the specialized organelles used to conduct chemical reactions necessary for the cell to function, such as communication, waste disposal, nutrition, repair, and reproduction. Organelles include things like the mitochondria (provide energy), endoplasmic reticulum (transport system), ribosomes (produce proteins), etc., each having their own specific function to keep the cell alive.

- This organization of the cell is often referred to as a factory where all of the organelles are the machines on the factory floor. Just as one could not look at a working factory and assume there is no manager to organize the machines and determine which machine produces what product when, one could not look at a cell and think there was not a designer to design each organelle to produce its specific product at the appropriate time. If the cell were only comprised of mitochondria, then it could not continue to live. Something established the perfect mix of each organelle type so that all of the necessary functions could be performed in order to keep the cell alive.

- It could also be compared to the organization of a sports team. If there were no coach to assign each player to their position, it would be pure chaos and the game would surely be lost. The coach, or the "designer," must lay out the plan for who is responsible for what function.

The cell's organization indicates structure and order, not randomness. It indicates a designer giving a cell this specific design and the specific components needed to accomplish its purpose.

Even that purpose is unique to each cell. A liver cell will only produce additional liver cells, but never a kidney cell. Lung cells will produce lung cells, but not muscle cells. Somatic cells are the exception and can produce any type of cell—yet the organism's DNA knows how many of each type of cell are necessary to produce that specific and complete organism. So not only is organization required within the cell, but it is also required within the organism for reproduction. Something must be directing the somatic cells to generate the appropriate number of each cell type in order to correctly reproduce an organism.

The third major component of the cell is the **nucleus**. The nucleus is the control center of the cell that contains the genetic information for the replication of the cell. The DNA in our cells stores that genetic data chemically. It is estimated that the information contained in a simple cell is around one **trillion** bits of data.[17]

*Where did that information come from?* Information cannot appear out of nothingness. A person can't just decide they know enough to be a brain surgeon. If one wanted to do that, they would have to gain that information from a source. Just considering the DNA molecule with its staggering amount of information, one could not say that a cell came into existence by random chance and without an intelligent designer behind it. But not only does the cell just have all of that information, it has all of that information stored in **code.**

*E.H. Andrews, Professor of Materials in the University of London says, "It is not possible for a code, of any kind, to arise by chance or accident…. A code is the work of an intelligent mind. Even the cleverest dog or chimpanzee could not work out a code of any kind. It is obvious then that chance cannot do it…. Codes do not arise from chaos."*[18]

Going back to the critical question to answer: is it more logical that the genetic code contained in DNA arose from a random, undirected chaotic process or from an intelligent organized source? Logic tells us that code does not come from chaos; therefore, logic should tell us that something more intelligent than the Big Bang Theory generated life. What is the logical presumption of fact?

The basic building block of all living things, the cell, is amazingly complex. It shows organization with multiple components performing individual functions to keep the cell alive. It is indicative of design, not randomness. Randomness cannot stumble upon highly ordered organization, but a designer can.

*Design of the Protein*

We'll now dig even deeper down into the basic elements of all cells, which is the **protein**.

Proteins carry out all of the essential activities in the cell on which the life of the cell depends. Each protein molecule is a long chainlike polymer made up of a linear sequence of amino acids. This is the *primary structure* of the protein. Each chain is somewhere between 100 and 500 amino acids long, and there are twenty-one amino acids found in living cells. That gives us somewhere between $21^{100}$ and $21^{500}$ possible permutations of amino acids!

Based on the different amino acids present and their sequence, the protein will fold first into a pleated sheet (*secondary structure*) and then again into a 3-D shape (*tertiary structure*). This shape is what determines the protein's specific functions. This 3-D shape also creates what is known as an active site. This site is where a specific enzyme will precisely fit, just like a lock and key, in order to perform a specific chemical reaction. And just like a lock where only the correct key will fit, only the correct enzyme will fit into the specific active site of that specific protein.

Consider then what happens if there is a genetic mutation. If one of those amino acids is wrong or missing, then it affects the protein chain, which changes the pleated shape, which alters the 3-D shape, which distorts the active site. With a changed active site, the mating enzyme can no longer fit to the protein and the protein cannot perform its function. If the protein cannot perform its function, then the cell cannot function. The sequence of amino acids must be precisely correct in order for the protein to work and for the cell to stay alive. We see this amazing level of precision even in the smallest element of all life.

*Formation of the Protein*

Not only is the protein chain amazingly precise, but the formation of a protein is highly complex as well.

Our DNA holds the master blueprints for protein creation. Messenger RNA then copies that information (known as transcription) from the DNA strand and carries it to the ribosomes. The ribosomes translate the code into a linear sequence, or chain, of amino acids that make up a specific type of protein with a specific function. To do that, the ribosome reads the RNA bases, or letters, in groups of three from the RNA strand. This triplet of letters is known as a codon. And every codon represents a specific amino acid. When the ribosome reads that codon, it translates it into which amino acid needs to come next for the protein chain. The transfer RNA brings that specific amino acid to the ribosome and attaches it to the growing protein chain. When the chain is complete, it detaches from the ribosome and then automatically folds into its 3-D shape.

Now consider again the implication of a genetic mutation. What if one of those "letters" (or RNA bases) were missing? Think about what that would do to the triplet reading of codons by the ribosome. The entire protein chain would be incorrect, and the protein could not function. Therefore the formation of proteins must be precise and accurate in order to maintain the life of the cell.

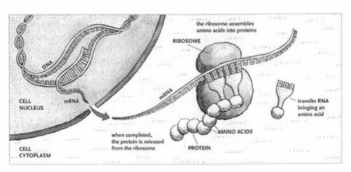

Protein Chain Synthesis[19]

However, the formation of proteins in the cell requires the integrated activities of nearly 100 different proteins, all carrying out different, very specific steps in the assembly of a new protein molecule. If any one of these did not exist, proteins could not be generated and therefore life could not be sustained. In other words, you have to have proteins in order to make proteins. We often jokingly ask, "Which came first, the chicken or the egg?" but it would be better to ask, "Which came first, the protein or the protein? Where did we get the first protein?"[20]

Could this process and the order of such a complex molecule that directs the basic functions of every cell have occurred randomly, by chance? The probability of a simple protein chain existing by chance is 1 in 10-with-125-zeroes.[21] Again, it is more logical to deduce that protein formation is the result of intelligent design and not from random chance. The presumption of fact tells us that there is a creator who designed this complex protein and this complex protein synthesis mechanism.

There is also an interdependence of the cell membrane and proteins.[22] Proteins are formed via a protein synthetic apparatus. This cannot function unless there is a cell membrane to hold its components together. The integrity of the cell membrane depends on the existence of a protein synthetic apparatus to generate the protein components of the membrane. One could not exist without the other.

Furthermore, the basic design of the cell is essentially the same in all living systems on earth, from bacteria to mammals.[23] The roles of DNA, messenger RNA, and protein are identical, and the meaning of the genetic code is virtually identical in all cells. So in terms of the basic biochemistry of cells, no living system can be thought of as being primitive or ancestral with respect to any other system. Yet the atheistic explanation for the existence of life and its complexities is that a simple cell happened by random chance and was slowly improved upon until it became a complex cell. But there is no "simple" cell that evolved to a "complex" cell, when all cells are equally complex. There is no simple version of a cell, where the complexities of protein formation, DNA code, and cell organization do not exist. There is an incredible level of complexity and precision in cells that could not have been reached through unorganized chaos.

If we can agree that computer code could not be randomly generated to execute a simple program, how can we think that proteins, RNA, and DNA could be randomly thrown together to execute the basic functions of a cell in order to sustain life? One must establish where the information contained in DNA could have originated. It becomes a probability problem. It is not probable that ordered, organized information was randomly created.

- If you were to stumble out onto the beach and notice a sequence of letters scribbled out on the sand, would you think that someone came along and wrote them? Would you think they appeared due to some random act of waves crashing on the sand?
- It would be even less likely if those letters were arranged in a very specific way so as to spell your name, and even less if your name was around 500 letters long.

A protein requires around 100 to 500 amino acid "letters" in order for our cells to carry out functions vital to life. Therefore, it is more logical to conclude that the cell and its components were designed. And if something shows design, then logically there must be a designer.

Irreducible Complexity

One way to describe the cell's protein synthesis process is by saying it is irreducibly complex. Irreducible complexity is a single system composed of several well-matched, interacting parts that contribute to the basic function, wherein the removal of any one of the parts causes the system to effectively stop functioning *in its intended manner.* Those are mechanisms that cannot be produced by continuously building up from a simple system by slight, successive modifications. Irreducibly complex systems must have all of the components of the system present, and working, all at the same time.[24]

> A simple way to illustrate this concept is by thinking about the mousetrap. A mousetrap is made up of five components: the platform, the hold down bar, the hammer, the spring, and the catch. The mousetrap depends critically on the presence of **all five** of its components in order to function.

One might say that the components by themselves could have some other purpose and therefore could be useful without the other components yet present; the platform alone could be a paperweight. But a paperweight is not a very good mice catcher. For the atheistic explanation to be accurate, it would presume that the platform alone would catch two mice per month. Through several generations of genetic mutations, the platform acquires the hold down bar and it now catches four mice per month. Repeat the process to add the spring, and now it can catch six mice per month, and so on. However, if there were no spring, the mouse would not be pinned to the base; if there were no platform, the other pieces would fall apart; and so on. The function of the mousetrap requires all the pieces working together at the same time.

The mousetrap cannot be an improvement on a simple design because it does not catch any mice at all until all five parts are present, sized accordingly, and integrated correctly. The point is that all components must be present at the same time for it to work in its *intended function.* All of the components of the mousetrap have to be in place before any mice are caught at all. Thus, the mousetrap is irreducibly complex.

Of course one must wonder what a mousetrap has to do with the existence of God. In the materialistic mindset (a world with no God), everything complex must be explained by the buildup from something simple that improved gradually over time. However, if some things are complex from the outset, then it means it could not have arisen from natural means only.

If the mechanism could not be reached by natural means, then it must have been reached by intentional design. The complexity of those mechanisms requires a designer to be behind it. Those complex things had to have been designed that way. And a design indicates a designer. Going back to the mousetrap example, all five components had to be designed in their appropriate size, shape, and integration in order for any mice to be caught. It was not incrementally built up from something simple. It was designed that way from the beginning.

*So, is there evidence of irreducibly complex mechanisms in nature?*

*Bacterial Flagellum*

The bacterial flagellum is a whiplike appendage that protrudes from the bacterium. Its primary function is transportation. The bacterium uses the flagellum to propel itself through its environment. The flagellum is made up of a protein that is shaped like a hollow tube with a sharp bend just outside the bacterium's outer membrane. A shaft runs between this bend and the base, passing through protein rings in the cell's membrane that act as bearings. The bacterial flagellum is driven by a rotary engine made up of proteins, powered by a flow of protons across the bacterial cell membrane. The rotor transports protons across the membrane and is turned in the process. The direction of rotation then can be switched almost instantaneously by reversing that flow of protons. It can even vary the rotational speed of the flagellum based on the intensity of the proton flow.

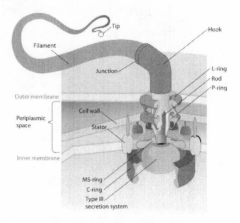

Bacterial Flagellum[25]

The use of the flagellum is critical for the life of bacteria. Bacteria must be able to move rapidly towards attractants and just as rapidly away from repellants. Otherwise, the bacterium would cease to exist. In terms of Darwinian evolution then, it would have only one generation to get the design of this flagellum right. It could not survive to the next generation if this mechanism were not functioning properly at the outset.

However, the design of the bacterial flagellum is analogous to an engine, only it is more energy efficient and can change directions instantaneously. Remove any of those components— rings, bearings, shafts, and rotors (even the same terms as a man-made engine)—and the flagellum would cease to function. Just like a man-made engine, all of the components must be present together at the same time in order for it to function. It could not have arrived by the slow, gradual buildup of parts from something simple to become something complex. In other words, the bacterial flagellum is an *irreducibly complex* mechanism. This is evidence of design, and a design requires a designer.[26]

*Blood Clotting Mechanism*

The ability for your blood to clot when you are cut is critical to life. It is essential that your body be able to stop bleeding and heal itself at the appropriate times, yet still have blood flow freely internally to all your organs. The concept seems fairly simple, but the clotting of blood uses about a dozen proteins that are activated only when tissues or blood vessels are damaged. And these are all activated in a sequential fashion; so the first step, or factor, activates the second step, which then activates the third, and so on.[27]

Blood clots are made from fibers (polymers) of a protein called fibrin. Fibrin monomers come from an inactive precursor called fibrinogen. The fibrinogen molecule has caps on either end that mask fibrin-to-fibrin binding sites (much like the plastic strips on the Band-Aid sticky parts). If these sites were not protected in some fashion, then your blood would always be clotted, which causes issues for it flowing freely through your body.

When clots are necessary, these caps must be removed so that the fibrinogen molecule can bind to other fibrinogen molecules to form a clot. The enzyme thrombin converts fibrinogen to fibrin monomers. Calcium is then used to glue fibrin monomers together to form fibrin polymers. Multiple fibrin polymers join together in a loose meshwork by using clotting Factor XIII. This then traps blood cells and forms a clot to stop bleeding.

As clotting factors (Factor XIII) are taken away from the site of the injury by the bloodstream, they become inactivated by enzymes downstream. This ensures that clotting only occurs at the site of the injury and not further down the bloodstream. As the clot builds up, the increased presence of the fibrin polymers starts to inhibit the enzyme thrombin. Remember, thrombin is what is used to convert the fibrinogen to fibrin (taking off the plastic strips to the Band-Aid). So as thrombin is inhibited, it stops activating fibrinogen, which slows the formation of the clot.

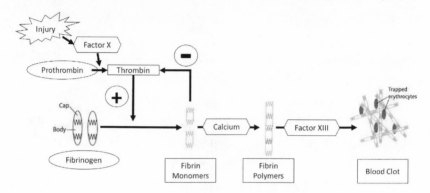

Blood Clotting Cascade

Once the clot is formed and your cut has healed, the clot must be destroyed. As the clot is being built up, it releases Tissue Plasminogen Activator (TPA), which converts plasminogen, an inactive precursor found in the blood, into plasmin. Plasmin is the enzyme used to dissolve clots. The amount of plasmin present is not very high, so the clot removal process is very slow, giving your cut time to heal.

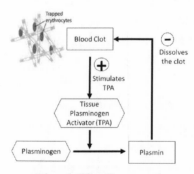

Blood Clot Removal

All of these genes, factors, and enzymes are necessary, working together in the system for blood clotting (and clot removal!) to be effective. But did they all come together at the same time, or could each gene and factor evolve into this mechanism independently? The materialist would say that each gene was acquired through a different evolutionary process to make the blood clotting mechanism more efficient. In other words, the organism would have only one of these genes present and then in the following generations evolve a second gene and so on until we have the completed chain of genes and enzymes that we see today. Is that possible? What is the presumption of fact?

There have been experiments conducted on lab mice to determine just such a thing.

- In the first group, researches removed the gene for plasminogen, so these mice **lacked the ability to remove clots**. In this scenario, the researchers were determining if mice could have only the ability to form clots (yet not dissolve clots) until another succeeding generation of mice evolved the gene for dissolving clots. The result was mice that could form clots but could not dissolve those clots. They exhibited thrombosis, ulcers, and high mortality—a feature that is detrimental to the idea of evolution. In other words, the mice were not going to survive to another generation until evolution could invent a way to dissolve clots.

- In the second group, the gene for fibrinogen was removed, so those mice **lacked the ability to form clots**. In this scenario, the researchers were determining if mice could survive without the ability to clot while having the ability to dissolve clots until another succeeding generation of mice could evolve the gene for forming clots. The result was the mice showed hemorrhaging and death in pregnancy—which is again detrimental to the idea of evolution. If the mice are unable to survive pregnancy because of the inability to form clots, then the mice are not going to have the chance to evolve the gene for producing clots in the next generation.

- The third group then had both genes removed. This would be the state of mice at the beginning of the supposed evolutionary chain, where **neither a gene for forming nor dissolving clots** was present. In this group, the mice exhibited the same characteristics as those that did not have fibrinogen. And this is what one would expect. The mice would suffer the same consequences as those without the ability to form clots rather than those without the ability to dissolve clots. They can't suffer the effects of undissolved clots if they are unable to form clots in the first place. This means that they exhibited thrombosis, ulcers, and high mortality—a feature that is detrimental to the idea of evolution.

Blood Clotting Factors in Mice[28]

| Lacking Plasminogen (unable to dissolve clots) | Lacking Fibrinogen (unable to form clots) | Lacking Both |
|---|---|---|
| - Thrombosis<br>- Ulcers<br>- High mortality | - No clotting<br>- Hemorrhage<br>- Death in pregnancy | - No clotting<br>- Hemorrhage<br>- Death in pregnancy |

The purpose of this experiment was to see if the genes could develop independently and be built up in small changes over time. What the experiment proved was quite the opposite. If you remove any one of these factors, then the blood clotting mechanism fails to work. The system had to develop all together, at the same time, and not as a buildup by a "random, natural" process. It is *irreducibly complex*; and yet it is a function highly critical to all forms of life. It shows evidence of design, and a design requires a designer.

*DNA Replication*

DNA replication is the most essential mechanism to the existence of life. If DNA could not replicate, cells could not replicate, and no further organisms could be created. Both the evolutionary model and the theistic creation model depend upon the success of DNA replication. But which model better predicts the existence of this mechanism?

DNA, or deoxyribonucleic acid, is the double-stranded helix that contains the genetic instructions used in the development, function, and reproduction of all known living organisms. It chemically stores all our biological information. Each strand of DNA is composed of a sugar, a phosphate group, and a nitrogenous base (adenine, thymine, cytosine, and guanine). The mating strand of DNA is made up of a sugar, phosphate group, and the mating nitrogenous base pair (adenine pairs with thymine, and cytosine pairs with guanine). The mating strand of DNA actually runs in the opposite direction, or it is said to be antiparallel. One side of the DNA goes in the 5' to 3' direction, determined by the orientation of the sugar molecule, and is known as the leading strand. The other side goes in the 3' to 5' direction and is known as the lagging strand.

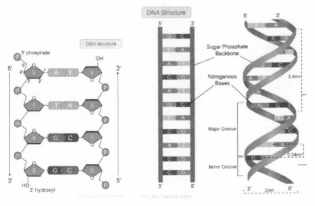

DNA Structure[29]

DNA replication must begin by separating the two strands of DNA. The enzyme helicase is used to basically unzip the DNA to prepare for replication. Once the DNA is unzipped, though, single stranded binding proteins are necessary to keep the open DNA molecule from reattaching to itself. These proteins are put in place to prevent any rebinding of the DNA strand. The enzyme DNA polymerase is then used to recreate each strand's complementary DNA sequence. However, DNA polymerase does not know where along the DNA strand to begin replication. So the enzyme primase, which is actually a piece of RNA, acts as the initializer to indicate to the polymerase where to start the replication process. DNA polymerase can then make the complementary strand by finding the correct base through complementary base pairing, and bonding it onto the original strand. Because it is highly critical for DNA polymerase to get this pairing correct, it has a proofreading capability built in to reduce any replication errors.

Interestingly, DNA polymerase can only work in one direction on the DNA leading strand, in the 5′ to 3′ direction. Since the lagging strand of DNA runs in the opposite direction (3′ to 5′), DNA polymerase must work in a segmented approach, replicating a few sections of DNA at a time where it can move in the appropriate 5′ to 3′ direction. This results in multiple DNA fragments, known as Okazaki fragments. Therefore, another enzyme, ligase, is necessary to effectively glue each of these fragments together to form an unbroken new strand of DNA.[30]

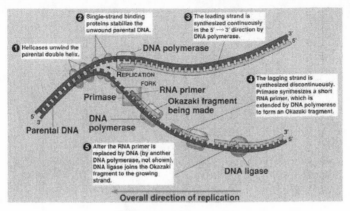

DNA Replication[31]

As you can see, the replication process of DNA is pretty complex and involves several key components in order for it to work. Even in this simplified explanation of the process, there are five different proteins that must work together. If any of these were missing, DNA could not be replicated. And DNA replication is critical to all life forms. If this process does not work, then cells could not reproduce. This would place quite a damper on any evolutionary process.

So again, we find another life critical process that is better defined as an *irreducibly complex* mechanism. All of the components—DNA, helicase, polymerase, primase, ligase, and single stranded binding proteins—must have been fully formed and fully functional **before the first cell could replicate**. *How could the evolutionary model ever have resulted in this mechanism?*

This isn't just a mechanism that must work, but it must work with **absolute precision** for life to continue. The fact is that evolution, a materialistic explanation, cannot account for this kind of complicated process with multiple working parts to that level of accuracy and consistency that is necessary for life.

The flagellum, the blood clotting cascade, and DNA replication are just a few of many examples of systems in biology that could not be built up by small steps in the fashion of the Darwinian Evolutionary Theory. Those systems are irreducibly complex, yet each of them performs a function highly critical to all forms of life.

Why does this matter? What is the importance of showing something is irreducibly complex?

If we observe something complex that cannot be built up by small, incremental improvements on something simple, then it could not be explained by only natural causes. It is evidence of design, and design must have a designer.

*Darwin once wrote, "If it could be demonstrated that any complex organ existed which could not possibly have been formed by numerous, successive, slight modifications, my theory would absolutely break down."*[32]

Conclusion

Going back to our initial question for this lesson: *is there evidence of design in our universe?* We have shown that the universe has specific attributes that provide for and sustain life. We examined the precision and accuracy found with the protein and cell— the most basic elements of all life. And we described multiple examples of irreducibly complex systems found in biology that are vital to life.

It is improbable that these things came about with such precision, all at the same time, by a random process born out of chaos. These things had to be designed with each component uniquely designed with its distinctive function, and each component integrated with the other components for a working system.

Just like on a factory floor, each machine is incredibly complex on its own. And each machine has been designed with its own function and purpose to specifically complement and enhance the unique functions of the other machines in order to generate a product. No one would try to assert that a factory producing highly precise computer products was the result of a tornado through a trailer park. Nor should we look at the complexity and design within the universe and the precision of the cell and think it came from a random explosion in space and blind, mutative processes.

While we've discussed several complicated examples, the great thing is you only have to provide **ONE** example of something designed to require the existence of a designer. You could have thousands of examples of things developing at random, but once you have one instance of something ordered, planned, or designed, there must be a designer because order does not arise from chaos.

This is the second argument of four that we will make to show that there must be a God because there must be a Designer.

**QUESTIONS FOR CONSIDERATION**

Why is it necessary to show design in the universe?

How do we know there is still a designer if there are examples of non-design?

Why is it statistically unlikely that random processes resulted in our universe?

How does the complexity of the cell indicate that there is a designer?

What are some biological functions that are impossible to get right through the evolutionary process?

The precision found in the mechanisms of protein synthesis and DNA replication contradicts the idea that they originated out of randomness. How does this establish the presumption of fact that God exists?

Why does the materialistic explanation require that everything complex is the result of the buildup from something simple?

Why is it important to show that something is irreducibly complex?

What are other examples of irreducibly complex systems found in nature?

# LESSON 3

## The Anthropological Argument

**INTRODUCTION**

Over the past two lessons we have discussed two different arguments that a creator of some kind must exist. The first lesson showed that the universe is a finite material entity that is not eternal. It is therefore an effect and must have some adequate cause. The cause could not have been the effect, or the universe itself, so something outside of this finite universe must have created us. The second lesson showed that this universe has been uniquely and amazingly designed. The earth is uniquely placed in the universe and has the exact physical parameters necessary for life to exist here. There is amazing precision in the cell and the protein, of which all life consists. The bacterial flagellum and the processes of protein synthesis, DNA replication, and blood clotting are examples of irreducibly complex designs found within nature. None of those life-critical mechanisms could have arisen through the slow, gradual buildup from a simple structure. They had to be designed with all of those working parts in place at the same time in order for life to continue. Those things are evidence of design, and design indicates there is a designer.

The cosmological argument and the teleological argument are two ways to logically and scientifically deduce with a presumption of fact that a God must exist to cause our universe and to design our universe. The next argument will look at philosophy and humanity to show that there is more to us than just physical components. And something more than physical components must have given that to us.

**STUDY**

Mind vs Matter

We oftentimes hear phrases like "It has a mind of its own" or "Mind over matter." *What do we mean when we use the term "mind"?* When we say that we have a mind, we are typically referring to our consciousness. It encompasses what we are aware of when we introspect.[1]

If you've ever had an operation, then you have experienced that moment when you regain your mind, or consciousness. It's when you ask yourself, "Where am I? What's going on?" And then you remember you were operated on, that your body hurts, and that you're in the hospital.

It consists of sensations, thoughts, emotions, desires, beliefs, and free choices that make us alive and aware. Our minds are what give us our essence of existence. Philosopher René Descartes described it as, "I think, therefore, I am." But where does that thinking come from? Is our mind the same thing as our brain? Did we evolve, through a natural, mechanistic process, into thinking, living creatures?

And *why does this discussion even matter*? If the mind and the brain are the same, then they are both material entities. Thus, if our minds came strictly from matter, then the awareness we have of our existence could possibly be explained through materialistic means alone. However, if our minds are separate from our brains and cannot be generated from matter, then the existence of our minds must be explained somehow.

There are two theories that attempt to address the existence of the mind and the brain.

1.   Dualism. We are both mind and brain. The Biblical perspective would support this idea. Both the Old Testament and New Testament consistently teach that we are a "hyphenate creature, a spirit/body dichotomy."[2] The formation of Adam in Genesis is stated as the result of the animation of a body by a spirit, constituting it as a living soul.

Jesus describes the body and soul as being distinct from one another. When He is hanging on the cross, He tells the thief that he would be with Him in paradise indicating the body would die but the soul/spirit would not (ref. Luke 23:43). Jesus also said in Matthew 10:28, "And do not fear those who kill the body but cannot kill the soul." Paul describes this dualism in 2 Corinthians 5:8 that to be absent from the body is to be present with the Lord.

2.   Physicalism.[3] The brain is matter only; it creates thoughts and nothing more. We are nothing more than physical matter generating thoughts. Darwinian evolutionists believe that once the brain reached a certain level of structure and complexity, people became conscious—that is, they suddenly developed subjectivity, feelings, hopes, a point of view, self-awareness, introspection, or that "hidden voice of our private selves." For the physicalist,

our minds are just evidence of superior evolutionary progress.

Only one of these models can be true, so we have to determine which of these models is correct. One way to do that is by assessing the consequences from each model. If the results from each model are valid, then it lends credibility to the base assumptions of that model. Consider the results from the model of physicalism. If physicalism were true:

1. Consciousness wouldn't really exist.[4] If everything were matter, then everything could be described by physical things from the third-person point of view. Everything in matter can be captured on a graph—you could locate each star, the moon, Susie's kidney, Johnny's brain, and so on. Everything would be explained entirely in third-person.

However, we do have a first-person description of certain things. We have subjective points of view, personal experiences, thoughts, and emotions. Therefore not everything is just a physical explanation.

2. There would be no free will.[5] If our mind were just an evolution of matter, then all the things we do would be fixed by our matter and our environment. You could have no free will to rise above your material components. We would simply have a programmed response to certain physical stimuli.

Dr. Wilder Penfield conducted experiments to study just this kind of response and interaction between the mind and the brain. He electrically stimulated parts of the brain to move certain body parts. The body parts were therefore moving only as a physical response to an outside stimulus.

Yet the patients made a distinction between what they did (what they chose to do) and what the doctor did (movement as a result of only physical stimulus and not the will of the patient).[6]

Dr. Penfield concluded, "The patient thinks of himself as having an existence separate from his body."[7] He also said, "There is no place [no matter how much he probed the cerebral cortex] where the electrical stimulation will cause a patient to believe or decide."[8] That's because those things originate in the conscious mind and not the brain. There was always a distinction between the physical response to stimulus and the free will of the patient.

If there were no free will, then we could never be held personally responsible for our actions. That point is critical to understand and is possibly the driving reason for making the mind just be a part of matter. If there is nothing more to our mind than just genetics and physical responses to our environment, then we don't have a choice about anything we do. Therefore, we could never be held personally accountable for our actions. Understandably, our genetics do make up a great deal about how we act and respond to things, but it is not the only thing that does. People undergo counseling, therapy, or rehab in order to teach themselves to act and react differently than how they are physically predisposed to behave. While this may not always be successful, it speaks to our understanding that many times we do have the choice to behave differently from what our genetics or environment dictate.

In fact, we quite often **do** make choices contrary to our genetics and physical stimuli from our environment. We have souls, desires, feelings, and beliefs that drive us to do things even though we may suffer from it. It's what causes us to push through pain to achieve some goal or withstand some pain for a greater cause (picture William Wallace's cry of "FREEDOM!" in *Braveheart*). The will of a person is a powerful thing, powerful enough to overcome tremendous circumstances. There is clearly something inside of us that pushes us beyond just our material existence.

3. The brain would have all the same characteristics of the mind.[9] Our thoughts have the attributes of being true or false. The thought that "The sun rises in the east" can be either true or false. However, our brain as physical matter can't be in a state of "true" or "false." So there are characteristics that our consciousness has that our physical brains do not. Therefore, they can't be the same thing.

4. Scientists could study the mind directly.[10] We have thoughts that are inner and private only to ourselves that can't be observed by anyone else. While a doctor can study your brain and see when synapses are firing or different lobes are lit up, it still doesn't mean the doctor knows our minds. A synapse firing in your brain cannot reveal to the doctor that you desire to be a teacher one day. The doctor can know everything that's happening in your *brain* but not everything that's happening in your *mind*.

One example is in the studies done on REM sleep, or Rapid Eye Movement. A scientist can see REM and know that something is going on with your brain. But to know that correlated to someone dreaming, the doctor had to ask the patient what they were doing—because the dream is in the mind. He can study the brain, but he has to ask about the mind.

We even understand this in our common vernacular. We can't get to know someone through studying their body. That's why we always hear the phrase, "Get inside someone's head." We can see someone's physical self, but we have to get them to reveal to us their thoughts, their emotions, their desires, or their worldview in order to really know who they are. We are making the distinction between a person's physical matter of their brain and the essence of who they are as a person in their mind.

5. <u>We could not trust any theoretical thinking.</u>[11] If our minds did arise solely from material particles put together at random, then we could not trust any thoughts that came out as a result. For example, if you found a calculator that was randomly assembled by monkeys, would you trust it to do your calculus homework? Likewise, if minds are just an evolution of matter only, then we should not trust the workings of *any* mind. Theoretical thoughts can't evolve to be trustworthy because theoretical thinking does not contribute to survival value.

Considering the consequences from the physicalism model, we can deduce that it is not a logical conclusion that the brain and mind are the same. They cannot both be material entities. Clearly, we would live in a very different world than we see today if we are only a result of physical matter with only the brain and no mind. There would be no free will, no consciousness, and no theoretical thinking. Yet we do exhibit all of those things so we have to conclude that physicalism is not an accurate model to explain the awareness of our existence.

Furthermore, if the mind and the brain were the same thing, then eventually you could physically dissect a person until you could discover their thoughts and opinions. But no matter how much you were to physically dismantle a person atom by atom, you'll never be able to discover what that person desires to do the rest of the day, or how they feel about the president, or what they believe in their religion. The mind is different from the brain.

There is more to us as people than just the physical entity of our brains.[12]

Now that we know the mind is different from the brain, we have to wonder *how we could get to a mind if there were no God.* How could we get something totally different—conscious, living, thinking, feeling, and believing creatures—from materials that don't have that? You can't get something from nothing. If there were no God, then the history of the entire universe would be a history of dead matter with no consciousness. We would not have any thoughts, beliefs, feelings, sensations, free actions, choices, or purpose. It would just be one physical event after another with everything behaving ONLY according to the laws of physics and chemistry, simply responding to different environmental stimuli.[13]

According to the two models of origins, there is either "in the beginning was a particle" or "in the beginning was the *Logos*" (or divine mind). If you start with particles (as in Darwinian fashion), you will only continue to get a rearrangement of different physical particles.[14] You will never get a *logos*, the mind or consciousness. You can't get a mind to come out of dead, mindless matter. However, if you start with the infinite mind, then you can explain how minds and particles can come into existence.

Christianity starts with God: "In the beginning, God." God is conscious; God has thoughts, beliefs, desires, and purpose. Therefore, we have no trouble explaining the origin of the human mind and consciousness. From that beginning, we can deduce that God is:

1. Rational, intelligent, creative, and aware—because *we* are rational, intelligent, creative, and aware. The Creator cannot give to the creation something that it does not have.
2. Invisible—because the conscious is invisible. We aren't able to "see" God in the same way that we aren't able to "see" one another. We see other people's bodies but not

who they are. We can't physically take apart one another and see them, their soul, their mind, or their desires. We are equally invisible to one another as God is invisible to us. We only see a physical representation of who we are on the inside in our spirit.

3. Omnipresent—our souls occupy our entire body and not any one particular part of it. Your soul is not in your lungs, your heart, your brain, nor your feet. Your soul is all of you, fully present, everywhere. If you have a heart transplant, you don't lose your soul. If you lose a body part, you do not lose your soul because it exists throughout all of you. In the same way, God occupies space. If you cut space in half, you wouldn't lose half of God.[15]

And this is what we should expect. We are made in God's image. So shouldn't there be parallels between us and God?

So ponder on this (and by pondering you will affirm that you have introspection apart from electrical firings in your brain): You *are* a soul, and you *have* a body. You think, therefore God is, as a reformed way of looking at Descartes.[16]

We see that we have a mind that is different from our matter. That explains our thoughts. But what really drives our actions?

## Anthropology

Anthropology is the study of humanity, including morality (the conformity to ideals of right human conduct) and ethics (the standard by which our attitude or actions are determined to be either right or wrong).

Nearly all aspects of human life can be boiled down to this field of study. All things have an ethical component to them.

- Academically, we expect scientific results to be reported honestly.

- Socially, we blame things on the breakdown of certain moral structures, like the family.
- Personally, we declare certain tragedies as things that ought not be.
- Religiously, we question why God allowed something to happen to us.[17]

This unintentional appeal to morality is common among all people. Atheists, Muslims, Christians, and Hindus alike use the terms "ought to," "ought not to," "unfair," and "fair." We hear them from adults and children, educated and uneducated. Interestingly, these remarks are made not just because the other person's behavior does not appeal to us and our personal preferences, but because we're appealing to some kind of standard of behavior which we expect the other person to know about.[18]

When someone is being told they are "unfair" or "ought not to" do something, the person rarely says they disagree with the standard of behavior, but rather they try to justify how they may *not* have violated that standard. Or if they did violate the standard, that there was some excuse for it.

We may say we were only short tempered with a friend because we were tired. In that statement we admit that we did indeed violate some standard of behavior by snapping at our friend. We acknowledge that it is not right to snap back at someone, we're just providing some excuse for it.

As for how we treated our spouse/children/friend/teacher, if folks only knew just how irritating they were being, then they would excuse that behavior, too.

Even someone who has completely abandoned any adherence to ethics or laws, such as a murderer on death row, will still view things as being unfair with regard to the way people ought to treat them. Someone may claim they don't believe in a right and a wrong, but eventually they will want to instill that rule if someone breaks that rule against them.

What this illustrates is that both sides of the argument have in mind some kind of rule or law of behavior for playing fair. *If we do not believe in decent behavior, then why should we be so anxious to make excuses for not behaving decently?*[19] It means we are forced to believe in a real Right and Wrong somewhere that all mankind is aware of. It means that Right and Wrong are not just a mere taste and opinion any more than the periodic table of elements is.

We can get two points from this:

1. That human beings all over the earth have this idea that they ought to behave in a certain way, and
2. That they do not in fact behave in that way.

This standard is referred to as the "Law of Human Nature" because it was thought, as a whole, everyone knew it by nature and no one needed to be taught it. Note that this is different from the "Law of Nature." For laws of nature, such as gravity, we don't really have a choice about obeying or not. However, we do have a choice in the matter of following the law of human nature. We all may be aware of this standard, but we still have a choice about behaving according to the standard. This law is unique not only because we have a choice but because we feel a compulsion about which choice *should* be made. This unique law of behavior is what separates us from the animals, plants, and inorganic material—it is a law with a choice and a compulsion.[20]

*What does this look like in our everyday lives?*

We know that it would be beneficial to us to cheat on a test when we didn't study, or to tell a lie when the truth makes us look foolish, or to break a promise when it's difficult to keep, but there is something that prevents us from doing these things. It's because we recognize those behaviors as being wrong. The Law of Human Nature, also known as the Moral Law, is what makes us adhere to the right behavior because we recognize the others as being wrong.

If we all exhibit this understanding of right behavior of honesty, loyalty, and unselfishness, then the existence of this law must be explained somehow. Since mankind is unique in having this Moral Law, *how did mankind acquire it*?

Is it a "law" just because that's the type of behavior that would benefit society?

This is a valid consideration. Society tends to benefit when people treat each other according to this standard. But that's essentially saying that we should behave decently for the benefit of society. Behaving decently to benefit society is behaving unselfishly; and behaving unselfishly is behaving decently. We've now created circular logic. We are still unable to define what decent behavior really is. It's like saying 'Men ought to be unselfish' because it benefits society. But we're trying to define what drives the "ought" part of that statement.[21] From where did man get the compulsion to benefit society? *Yes, we should behave to benefit society, but why?* This argument fails to explain the origin of the Moral Law. It simply points out its usefulness.

Is the Moral Law simply for limiting behavior that brings us harm?

It is apparent that most violations of the Moral Law actually harm another person. Someone is lied to, or betrayed, or physically injured when people violate this standard of behavior. However, there are times when something may bring us harm but we don't consider it indecent behavior or a violation of the Moral Law.

Likewise, there are times when something does not harm us but we do consider it indecent behavior.

For example, if someone accidentally trips you, it may cause you bodily harm but you don't consider that indecent behavior. However, if someone intentionally tried to trip you but did not succeed, you would consider that indecent, even though it brought no harm to you.

In the same way, you don't get mad at someone for sitting in the best seat on the bus when he got there first. But you get mad if he slipped into the seat while you were getting your bags. The end result is the same—we don't get the best seat on the bus—but we only consider it a violation of the Moral Law in the second scenario.[22]

Therefore, the Moral Law cannot only be limiting behavior to avoid pain for other people. There is something underlying about our intentions or our drive to do good. Saying it is simply to avoid harm fails to answer the question of where the Moral Law originates.

Is the Moral Law an instinct?

Since this compulsion for doing good usually comes from inside us, one might think this is just an instinct found in nature or something just inherited. We have other instincts inherited simply as being part of the animal kingdom, such as our mothering instinct or the instinct for finding food. But the Moral Law is much different from that.

Consider the scenario that you go for a walk in the woods and see a man fall into a river. It is obvious that the man cannot swim and is in grave danger. He begins to cry out for help. You have two instincts occurring:

1) An instinct or desire to help the man in need (herding instinct). It is a person after all who needs help and he probably has family and friends who would miss him.

2) An instinct or desire to run away (self-preservation). That water is really cold and the current is very strong. Besides you'd have to climb down a cliff to get to the water's edge, and you're not the best swimmer anyway.

*Which one do you choose?*

At that moment, along with those two instincts, inside of all us there will be a third feeling that tells you what you *ought* to do. It will say that you ought to go help this man. This third feeling will then work to suppress the self-preservation feeling to enable you to go help the man.

But this third thing that judges between the first two instincts can't then itself be one of the instincts. It must be above the two instincts, or outside of it, in order to judge.

It would be like saying a sheet of music used to tell you which note to play at what time is, in fact, a note itself. The sheet of music cannot be a note—the thing that tells you what note to play can't be a note itself.[23]

This third thing does not necessarily always go with the stronger instinct either. I'm sure the instinct for personal safety would be much stronger than saving a drowning man, yet we still act on saving the drowning man. The Moral Law is what compels you to help the drowning man above your stronger desire to save yourself. It tells you what you ought to do. We sometimes even have to stir up our imaginations and arouse our pity to get up enough steam for doing the right thing. We focus more on the loss of his family than on the inconvenience to us to jump in the raging river. Clearly at that point we are not acting from instinct when we go about making an instinct stronger than it naturally is. The thing that tells you to encourage and "wake up" your herd instinct can't itself be your herd instinct.[24]

Another way to think about it is this. If the Moral Law was one of our instincts, then we should be able to point to one desire, or impulse, within us that is always considered good or decent behavior. The Moral Law is, after all, concerned with good behavior. But we know that none of our impulses are considered good at all times. We can't select any one instinct as the instinct to follow at all times at any cost. Every instinct at some point will need to be suppressed by the Moral Law, even though we may see that instinct as good.

> The mothering instinct cannot always be good (never suppressed) and the fighting instinct always bad (always suppressed). There are times when the Moral Law would have to suppress the mothering instinct—for the good of your child so they aren't spoiled. And there are times when the Moral Law would have to encourage the fighting instinct—for the good of national safety during wartime.

> Looking back to our piano example, every note is right at one time and wrong at another; it's not the note itself that tells us that but the sheet of music. The Moral Law is not any one note or instinct but the sheet of music that tells us when the right note or instinct should be played at the right time in order to make music or good behavior.[25]

Therefore, if the Moral Law can arouse some instincts and suppress others at their appropriate times, then the moral law is not an instinct.

## Is the Moral Law just something we're taught?

Even if it were something taught to us from our parents, you have to continue to trace it back to *somewhere*. It can't have come from our parents indefinitely. The first generation of parents would have to get these rules of behavior from somewhere.

Furthermore, people who ask that question are assuming that if we have learned a thing from our parents (or teachers), then that thing must be merely a human invention. That is not the case here. We all were taught the multiplication tables as a child from someone. But that does not mean it was invented by man. Nor does it mean it could have been any different if man had chosen to make it so. We have learned the law of gravity, but that does not mean the law of gravity was invented by man.[26]

The Moral Law is not just a human convention that could have just as easily been made differently, like which side of the road we drive on. Human conventions like that may differ to any extent from culture to culture. The Moral Law, however, is essentially the same throughout every culture.

*How can we say that when we see how morally depraved some cultures are?* It is true that morality takes a different shape in different societies, but we have to consider what a totally different moral base would involve. It would be a place where people were admired for running away during a battle, or a man felt proud for double-crossing all his friends. It would be someone praised for what a great liar they are.

Looking at different cultures, ancient and modern, the **core** moral base of them are the same, or rather there are certain traits that are pervasive, even from a civilized society to a cannibalistic one. Every culture desires honesty, fairness, loyalty, and unselfishness. Those cultures may differ over to whom you should be unselfish or loyal, such as your family vs the government, but they never value violating the Moral Law.[27] ISIS may have a different idea of how to value one's life than other societies, but they still demand loyalty to ISIS from within their ranks.

The Moral Law is not just set up to benefit society or to prevent others from being harmed. It is not an instinct and it hasn't just been taught to us for every generation. *So how do we explain the existence of this Moral Law?*

*From Man*

Since the atheist does not account for God, he must rely on raw, inorganic matter to generate and *promote* morality. Without God, ethics and morality must originate from the mind of man. If man has invented morality, then we end up with as many moral and ethical systems as we have people. Most of them would conflict but all would have to be equally valid. It would be impossible to determine which set of man-developed ethics is superior to or better than another. No one could thrust their set of evolved moral truths over someone else's evolved moral truths since they all originate from man.

> We couldn't say that Hitler's moral code was wrong because his moral code was simply what his mind had devised. We couldn't rank civilized morality over savage morality, or Christian morality over ISIS morality. Each version of morality would have equal footing.

In light of that, *where does the atheist get the idea that any other society is evil?* If God doesn't exist, then you are unable to find an absolute moral law. Without God, man has no authoritative sense of what is essentially good and therefore what is essentially evil.[28]

*This point is summed up by atheist Kai Nielsen, "We have not been able to show that reason requires the moral point of view.... Pure practical reason, even with a good knowledge of the facts, will not take you to morality.*"[29]

The atheist will say that advanced reasoning has resulted in the best moral codes, but reason alone still can't tell you whether things ought to be or not. In other words, an assessment of the facts fails to tell you whether those facts *should* be so. We can't extract the "ought" from an "is."

Consider the crime scene of a murder. The scientific description of the event would be the same as the scientific description of a rock falling off a cliff. Nothing in the factual description would tell you whether the murder was wrong. The "ought" and "ought not" makes a value judgment above or outside of the scientific process.[30]

*As John Lennox states, "Science can tell you that if you add strychnine to someone's drink, it will kill them, but science cannot tell you whether or not you ought to put strychnine into your grandmother's tea."*[31]

This is the dilemma found in moral relativism. Relativism means that there is no universal truth or moral absolute. It says that all value systems are derived based on cultural or individual differences so each moral system is equally correct. It means what's right for me may not be right for you and that's okay. It makes morality subjective to one's opinion instead of objective outside of opinion. Subjective morality would say that something is right or wrong based on our personal feelings or preferences. Objective morality would say that something is right or wrong regardless of what people may think about it.

Objective morality means that even if everyone on earth were Nazis, what the Nazis did was still wrong; subjective morality would say it was not wrong as long as everyone preferred it. But those actions were objectively wrong regardless of what people felt about it or what people preferred.

Morally healthy individuals hold certain things to be objectively wrong. Even atheists rely on objective morality when they point out things like the Crusades and the Inquisition as being wrong. By doing so, they are asserting an objective morality. The Crusades were wrong regardless of what the Crusaders felt about it.[32]

Our culture today often uses subjective morality when discussing the issue of abortion. The common statement is "I wouldn't do it but I wouldn't tell someone else not to." That is the ultimate definition of subjective morality. They are saying something is wrong for them because of their preference but right for someone else based on another preference. However, subjective morality breaks down as we start comparing cultural rights and wrongs.

If one culture believes in slavery and another doesn't, does that make it right (consider societies in Africa today)? What about the abuse and oppression of women (consider Arab/Muslim nations)? Or what about abortion (our own culture)? We label those things as being wrong, but apart from God, we have no reason to say those are wrong.

*Philosopher Richard Rorty states it this way: "If moral imperatives are not commanded by God's will, and if they are not in some sense absolute, then what 'ought to be' is simply a matter of what men and women decide 'should be.' There is no other source of judgment."*[33]

If there is no other source of judgment, then we cannot deem anyone's sense of good and bad as being more right or more wrong than anyone else's. Yet we clearly do judge those things. Even though our liberal culture wants to have moral relativism, with no absolute Right or Wrong, they still stand in judgment of other cultures and institutions as being right and wrong. But if all moral codes are equal, as the relativist believes, then how can we say one society is better than another? We call people reformers or progressives when they are trying to improve society. *But improve to what*? Why is improvement necessary **unless** there is an Ultimate Right and Ultimate Wrong, or rather Ultimate Morality, that we are working to attain?[34]

Improvement implies moving towards something better. And if there is something better out there, then all moral systems cannot be equal. If we openly agree that some societies are better than others, then we are choosing one as being more right. The mere act of choosing between these moral codes for which one is better or more right implies that we are again appealing to a superior standard of moral law. We would be comparing them against a Real Morality.[35]

> For example, the reason why your idea of New York can be truer than mine is because New York is a real place. If "New York" just meant whatever town I'm imagining in my head, then neither of us could have a truer idea of the place than anyone else.

> In terms of morality, if we can say that our moral law is closer to Right than that used by the Nazis, then there must be something, some Real Morality for us to be closer to. If society has improved after the Civil Rights Movement, then that means there is a standard we have moved closer to.

If the Moral Law was based on each individual culture, then we could never point to another culture as being wrong. Therefore, the Moral Law could not have come from man.

*So could it have come from nature?* Is it something that came from being at the top of the evolutionary chain?

*From Nature*

Many atheists would claim that morality is a result of nature, either through observation or evolution. There are two flaws to this idea though. First, morality cannot be observed in nature; it is something uniquely human. And second, objective morality could not arise through evolution because there is no evolutionary advantage for it.

Some claim that morality can be observed in nature. But we must be particular about what we are actually observing. Animals and humans do share common behaviors. But there is something distinct that sets humans apart from the rest of the animal kingdom, and it comes from this unique Moral Law that only humans have. Animals and humans may have similar instincts, such as a herding instinct, a mothering instinct, or a feeding instinct. But at the same time, the animal kingdom displays other behaviors that would be abhorrent if allowed in the human race. Some male animals reproduce by taking any female it likes, oftentimes multiple females. Some animals kill their young to prevent a challenge to the alpha male. Yet those actions in the human world would not be deemed as moral. Even some societies that accept such behavior are judged as indecent, immoral, or not as progressed as those who do not. We would say that those things "ought not be so" (and by judging them, we reaffirm the existence of the Moral Law).

In reality, even the judgment of those actions is different between animals and humans. The lion eating its cub is not seen as immoral because, well, it's an animal. But a human doing so would be morally reprehensible. Therefore there is something that sets our standard of behavior apart from the rest of the animal world. This point is eloquently phrased by Mark Twain: "Man is the only animal that blushes. Or needs to."[36]

The second problem with the atheist explanation is that objective morality could not exist if it is only a result of evolution and survival of the fittest. Evolution would mandate that anything that progresses the species would be "good." It means if rape or infanticide progressed evolution, we could not declare it as wrong. There would be no evolutionary advantage to protect the disabled and elderly in our societies since they would be simply less fit to survive.

Consider the reality of the mindset of the Nazi efforts to exterminate certain ethnicities. They were trying to cleanse the "lesser" species to promote the "fitter" species for survival. This was humankind enacting Darwinian evolution. If morality were simply a result of evolution, then those efforts would have to be applauded not condemned. It simply was aiding the survival of the fittest. Yet we unmistakably denounce those actions as evil.

Charles Darwin even said: "If men were reared under precisely the same conditions as hive-bees, there can hardly be a doubt that our unmarried females would, like the worker-bees, think it a sacred duty to kill their brothers, and mothers would strive to kill their fertile daughters; and no one would think of interfering."[37] Yet even the moral relativist should find issue with a society that condoned that behavior.

The Moral Law could not have originated from the mind of man, and it could not have resulted from the process of evolution. The only option left for where we received morality would be from something outside of nature and outside of mankind.

*From God*

We have shown that there is this inherent idea of certain behavior that is unfair or wrong. In order to assess behavior as wrong, we must be aware of what behavior is right. And we are assessing these behaviors against this Moral Law. This Moral Law clearly exists and did not come from any natural means. Therefore, there must be a Moral Law Giver, something outside of nature that imparted this Moral Law onto mankind alone. It is the only way to explain the existence of a Moral Law. Only this Moral Law Giver, or God, can give us the sense of an Ultimate Right and Wrong that we are inherently continually striving toward. Only a moral code based on Godliness, not mankind's preferences, can provide us adequate motivation for living an ethical life and for judging against those who do not.

This moral awareness, the ability to distinguish between right and wrong, is only a part of us because we were made in God's image. God is perfect and holy and good; therefore, when we were made in His image, we were given knowledge of that perfection, holiness, and goodness. Due to our free will and our choice of sin, we fall very far from that level of goodness. But it is only due to that goodness from God that we can see a difference between right and wrong. And only because of this imparting of the Moral Law do we have this innate compulsion to do what is right and refrain from what is wrong.

This seems difficult to state when there may be many examples of atheists that act more morally upright than some theists. However, it is important to note, it is not the *belief* in God that is necessary for morality, rather it is the existence of God Himself that is necessary for morality.[38] Because God does in fact exist, we have been imparted with this Moral Law whether we believe in God or not.

Atheists are still made in God's image whether they believe in God or not. It is an inescapable fact that we have an understanding of fair play, and that is only due to the existence of a Morally Upright God.

The Moral Law is all about fair play, unselfishness, courage, honesty, etc. Therefore the Moral Law Giver must be very interested in people doing right, or being good. In that case, we would have to conclude that the Moral Law Giver is also good. Consequently, the Moral Law Giver must **unwaveringly detest behavior that violates the Moral Law, or else He cannot be good.** Therefore, **He must hate most of what we do.** And this is the terrible situation that we are in. There is this Moral Law Giver that imparts a sense of moral standards in us that we violate on a daily basis. *What can we possibly do about that?*

Now we can start to look at this Moral Law Giver from the Christian perspective. Christianity tells people to repent with a promise of forgiveness. But this means nothing to people who do not know they have done anything requiring repentance or forgiveness. It is only after you understand this Moral Law, the Power that exists behind that Moral Law, and that you have broken this Moral Law and put yourself against this Power that you can understand what Christianity is about.[39]

Conclusion

We are more than just physical matter. We all have desires and passions that drive us far beyond what our physical conditions dictate, whether from our genetics or our environment. There is something inside us that is what really defines who we are as a person. That essence of life within each of us is different from the molecules and compounds that constitute our bodies. If all that ever existed was dead, inorganic matter, we never could have reached this spirit element that we so clearly exhibit. There must be a Spirit that gave us those features. The adequate cause of the effect of a spiritual being must be a Spiritual Being itself.

Not only do we all have a spirit, but we all have an innate sense about how things ought to be. Though it is hard for us to define sometimes, we do know how we should and should not behave. What is it that gives us that concept of a right and wrong? It could not have come through nature because nothing else in nature exhibits a sense of morality. Nature acts on instinct. Yet this moral barometer inside us can't be an instinct itself since we use it to tell us which instinct to act upon. The moral code can't even be something that man generated for the benefit of society; otherwise, we could never judge one moral code as being better or morally superior to another. Yet we do judge other societies' standards. But what are we judging them against? It means that deep down we all acknowledge there is an ultimate standard of Right and Wrong that each society is striving towards.

We have this Moral Law inside of us. We could not have put it there ourselves—therefore, there must be a Moral Law Giver. The adequate cause for a moral code is a Moral Being. The Moral Law Giver is ultimately interested in goodness, justice, and right behavior so He must hate any behavior that isn't. Therefore, He must be offended with all that we do. The next lesson will address the solution for this human predicament.

## QUESTIONS FOR CONSIDERATION

Why is it important to determine if our mind is different from our brain?

What are the two theories to explain the existence of our mind?

How does our free will show that our mind is a separate entity from our brain?

What common phrase indicates all mankind has a standard of behavior when so many societies are uncivilized or immoral?

What is the flaw in saying the Moral Law exists to benefit society?

How do we know the Moral Law is not an instinct?

Why is it insufficient to think we only have a Moral Law because we were taught it?

How does our judgment of other societies prove there is a Moral Law and that it was not invented by man?

How is moral relativism problematic for people trying to progress society?

How do we know the Moral Law did not come from evolution?

Why does the existence of a Moral Law mean that the Moral Law Giver is good?

Do you think all men violate this Moral Law? Do you think that offends the Moral Law Giver?

# WHICH GOD IS IT?

John 14:6 Jesus said to him, "I am the way, the truth, and the life. No one comes to the Father except through me."

Acts 4:12 Nor is there salvation in any other, for there is no other name under heaven given among men by which we must be saved.

# LESSON 4

## Religious Exclusivity

### INTRODUCTION

Through multiple disciplines of science and philosophy, we have proven that a god must exist. There must be a Cause to account for the effect of the universe. There was a Designer that designed the precise parameters found within the universe and complex mechanisms found within biology. There must have been a Spirit to give humans a spirit and mind separate from just our physical bodies. There was a Moral Law Giver to give humankind the sense of morality that we all strive to meet. We are intelligent, loving, rational, spiritual beings, so whatever Created us must be intelligent, loving, rational, and spiritual. But there are many different ideas of god all around the world. Which god is it that created this universe? Who is worthy of our praise and devotion? *How do we distinguish the Christian God from all other religious deities? Is Christianity the only way to Heaven?*

## STUDY

Many people try to insist that all religions are equally valid, that we each have our path to Heaven. Other phrases often said are: "What works for you may not work for me but that's okay"; "Can't we all be right in our own way?"; and "As long as your path makes you happy; as long as you're sincere in what you believe."

One of the most common misconceptions at the root of these phrases is that all religions are basically the same. Most religions have common ideas on how to behave and how to treat other people, but that doesn't make them all the same. Comparing religions based on morality will show similarities because they all give guidance—don't kill, don't lie, don't steal—but this comparison means that religions have a common denominator, not common doctrine. In reality, all religions are superficially similar but fundamentally different.[1] The morality of a religion is not what distinguishes it from other religions. Religions must be compared in doctrine, things such as the origin of humanity, nature of sin, the characteristics of god, the meaning of life, and the nature of the afterlife. Compared on those points, it will become clear that all religions are not the same. In fact, it will show that no religion is the same as another.

So what we need to be asking is "What is the truth?" *Can we really all be right?*

## Contradiction of Religions

All religions cannot be true because all religions contradict each other.[2] Even relativism is self-contradictory. Stating "That's true for you but not for me" is the same thing as saying: it is true that there is no truth. Or, I sincerely believe that sincere belief does not make something true. It is self-contradictory to claim truth by stating there is no truth. And a philosophy that denies the possibility of truth is a philosophy that denies its own truth-claims.[3] So the basis of relativism (so many people believe so many different things) and the conclusion of relativism (so many things are true at the same time) are not equal assertions. The fact that people believe multiple things does not mean they are all true at the same time.

Another problem with the idea that all religions are the same is that it ignores a fundamental truth about reality: ideas have consequences. What you believe matters because it will affect what you do. To claim that all religions are essentially the same is to say that it doesn't matter what you believe as long as you're sincere—and this neglects the fact that you can believe something sincerely and be sincerely wrong. Hitler held his beliefs with much sincerity—that doesn't make them true.[4]

To further assess the contradictions between religions, we must consider logic from the Law of Non-contradiction. The Law of Non-contradiction states that something cannot be both true and not true at the same time when dealing with the same context.[5] So if two statements about one particular issue contradict each other, then only one of them is true or both of them are false.

> For example, if we are stopped at a stoplight, you say it is red and I say it is not red. It cannot be both red and not red at the same time. Therefore, one of us is right and the other is wrong. But those two statements cannot coexist. They cannot both be true in the same sense and at the same time.

> For a more concrete example, I say that 2 + 2 = 5 and you say 2 + 2 = 3. We can't both be right. So one of us is right and the other is wrong ... or we are both wrong. But we cannot both be right. The answer cannot be both 5 and 3.[6]

Therefore, truth by its very definition is **exclusive**. If truth does not exclude, then no assertion of a truth claim can be made. Any time you make a truth claim, you are stating that whatever is contrary to it is false. Truth therefore excludes all other options; truth excludes the false.[7]

> Back to our simple math problem, we are going to say that it is truth that 2 + 2 equals 4. By saying that is truth, it means that any other result you come up with for 2 + 2 is false. So the truth that the answer is 4 excludes any other answer besides 4.

In the terms of religion, all religions claim exclusivity because all claim to be the ultimate path to God. If you disagree, try to tell a Muslim that he is a Jew and see how he reacts. So looking at the Law of Non-contradiction, if I say salvation is through God's son and if a Muslim says God doesn't have a son, then we can't both be right. We have to be resigned to say that one of us is right or we're both wrong.[8] Even a claim that there is no exclusivity in religion (meaning they all accept and encompass one another) eliminates those religions who do claim exclusivity.

Typically, Christians are accused of being the exclusivists. But Christianity is not the only religion that excludes. Islam teaches that there is one unpardonable sin—to accept that God has a son. Christianity teaches that one must accept Jesus as the Son of God for salvation. Therefore, Islam excludes Christianity just as much as Christianity excludes Islam. Popular sects of Hinduism believe everything is god, but Christianity and Islam assert there is one true God, while Buddhism and atheism believe there is no god at all. Buddhism was founded when Gautama ("Buddha") rejected two fundamental assertions of Hinduism—the ultimate authority of the Vedas (their scriptures) and the caste system. Buddhism inherently excludes Hinduism, or any religion that claims there is a god. The fundamental tenet of atheism is that there is no god at all, which rejects all the religions discussed thus far.

Therefore, Buddhists don't believe in a god. Muslims don't believe Jesus was the son of God. Atheists don't believe there is a god at all—*so which kernel of truth can be taken from each of these so that they are not mutually exclusive?* It's possible that all of these religions are wrong, but it is not possible that all of them are right. Each one rejects the other. This establishes that we can't all be right. There has to be one TRUE religion that is based on TRUTH because they can't all be right at the same time.[9]

Three Major World Views

Since all religions exclude one another and all religions can't be true at the same time, one must then investigate the doctrinal truths about each religion to determine which one is really truth. To do that, one must look at the method of salvation, the goal of salvation, the leader (or revelation) of that salvation, and the text that is used in its accomplishment. The table below summarizes each major world religion, and the text that follows will discuss each in detail.

Comparisons of World Religions[10]

| | Hinduism | Buddhism | Islam |
|---|---|---|---|
| Method | Yoga, meditation | Follow the Eight-Fold Path on how to end suffering | Follow the Five Pillars |
| Goal/salvation | Deny reality and improve karma to reach a state where reincarnation stops (nirvana) | Eliminate desire to achieve deliverance (moksha), but not sure what eternal life brings | Only the most diligent achieve eternal life |
| Leader/Revelation | None | Buddha | Mohammed |

| Text | Smriti and Shruti | No main text; passed by word of mouth<br>- Buddha's teachings (sutras)<br>- Notebook for monks (Vinaya) | Quran |
| --- | --- | --- | --- |

*Method for Salvation*

Hinduism

The goal of Hindu salvation is to deny reality and embrace a spiritual reality that is defined as the belief that "all is god." Salvation is inseparable from a fundamental belief in karma and reincarnation. In order to obtain salvation, one must improve their karma. By getting rid of bad karma, one can transcend to a higher future existence. Once this higher level has been reached, salvation becomes a state of existence where one does not experience reincarnation. At that point the Hindu enters into a state of oneness with the Brahman. The Hindu then ceases to exist as an individuated human being, and this is known as nirvana. The way to achieve this is from understanding the human predicament through discipline, such as yoga, and devotion to one of the gods (especially Shiva).

Buddhism

The focus for Buddhists is to eliminate desire, which is the key to deliverance (moksha). Once desire has been eliminated, then the Buddhist can enter a state of nonexistence and cease to exist as an individual. The Buddhist must desire to eliminate desire.

Since Buddhism is a nontheistic system, ethics become the central part of the religion, and rules are added endlessly—all of which Buddha creates. As an example, one of the prayers for forgiveness from the Buddhist Common Prayer asks to be freed from the Four States of Woe, the Three Scourges, the Eight Wrong Circumstances, Five Enemies, Four Deficiencies, and the Five Misfortunes. The focus for the Buddhist is on right understanding, right speech, right effort, and right mindfulness through meditation and concentration.

The Buddhist begins with the Four Noble Truths on suffering and then follows the Eight-Fold Path on how to end suffering. Once a person enters the Eight-Fold Path, there emerge hundreds of other rules and contingencies. For example, Buddha provides thirty rules on how to ward off the pitfalls of committing one of the four offenses that result in a loss of one's discipleship status. Within those thirty rules, there are 92 rules that apply to just one of the offenses. There are 75 rules for those who are entering the order of Buddhism. There are 227 rules for men to follow to enter discipleship, and 311 rules for women. In fact, Buddha had to be persuaded to even allow women to enter discipleship status. He finally agreed to allow women as disciples, but decided to create additional rules for them.[11]

For salvation, the Buddhist believes that man lives his own fate and has no one to blame but himself. In a sense, there is eternal life, but one is not sure what his next life will end up being. It depends on the karma of his present life. The only thing that can help someone when facing death is their state of mind or the state of their mental and spiritual development.

According to Buddhist beliefs, each action by the Buddhist is laying down subtle imprints in the mind that can result in either future happiness or future suffering, depending on whether each action was positive or negative. These imprints will eventually determine one's future if they are not spiritually cleansed. And this is really what karma is. The Buddhist believes that at death the mind and body separate, and the mind takes with it all of those imprints from that life and any previous lives. The mind then wanders for up to seven weeks until a suitable place for rebirth has been found.

The key for the Buddhist then is the state of mind at that moment of death. If the mind is calm and peaceful with positive thoughts at the time of death, then this will direct the mind to a happy rebirth. However, if the mind is angry or fearful at the time of death, then it will direct it to an unhappy or lower rebirth. This is why meditation is so crucial for the Buddhist. They believe that the mind that arises at the time of death is the one the person typically demonstrates. Therefore, the time to prepare for death for the Buddhist is now. The Buddhist must continually train their minds to always be in a positive state. They want to develop control over their minds so that it will be free from fear and negativity at the time of death.[12]

Death for the Buddhist is still not a permanent existence though. Death leads to a rebirth in one of six realms: heaven, human beings, deities, ghosts, animals, or hell. The destination is determined by the accumulation of the Buddhist's karmic actions. None of those places are permanent though. Life for the Buddhist does not end—it just goes on in other forms.

Islam[13]

Muslims must strictly adhere to the laws dictated in the Koran and its faith rules. However, the faith rules of Islam actually have a lot of language in common with Christianity. It is important to understand the different connotations of these similar terms since there are vast differences between these two religions.

The first faith rule for the Muslim is to have faith in the oneness of Allah, meaning Allah alone with no other partners or associations. Christians would say they have faith in one God, but technically it is a triune God. Muslims do not believe in associating partners with Allah; therefore, belief in God the Father, God the Son, and God the Holy Spirit is polytheism to a Muslim.

The other distinction is that faith in Allah is just a mental acceptance of the existence of a very impersonal, unknowable god. This is why the second faith rule becomes extremely important. The Muslim must have faith in angels. Because Allah is unknowable, angels become the focal point as Allah's messengers. If you can't know the god, then you must know its messenger. After all, it was the angel Gabriel that revealed the truth to Mohammed. Faith in angels for the Muslim, therefore, is different from the Christian's simple belief that angels exist.

Muslims must also have faith in all of Allah's holy books, which include the Torah, Psalms, and Quran. Many Christians want to assert a commonality here because we have faith in the Bible just like the Muslims have faith in the Quran. However, the Quran has a very different significance to Muslims than the Bible does to the Christian. Muslims believe the Quran is the final revelation from Allah and is in fact how Allah is physically revealed. The Christian believes the Word became flesh in Jesus Christ, but the Muslim believes the Word became flesh in the Quran. That is why the Quran is so exalted by the Muslim. The analogy is actually that the Quran is to the Muslim as Jesus is to the Christian, not as the Bible is to the Christian.

The fourth faith rule is to have faith in all of Allah's prophets, including, among others, Noah, Abraham, Moses, Jesus (only as a prophet), and Mohammed. However, to the Muslim, all of these prophets are sinless. In the Bible, though, all of these prophets (except for Jesus) have evidence of a sin nature. This is why the Muslims believe the Bible has errors in it. To them, prophets are sinless. Since the Bible shows the prophets sinned, the Bible must be wrong.

The fifth faith rule is faith in the Day of Judgment. The preaching of hell is always front and center for the Muslim and is probably why they have such urgency for their actions against unbelievers. Lastly, the sixth pillar of faith is faith in destiny. Muslims believe Allah has ordained everything, which becomes the ultimate view on predestination. This is why Muslims tend to end statements for future activity with the phrase "if Allah wills." In addition to the faith rules, Muslims must also focus on prayer, paying charity, fasting for Ramadan, and pilgrimage to Mecca for those who can afford it.

Eternal life for the Muslim is defined as 'eternal bliss in the hereafter,' but final salvation is reserved only for the most diligent of Muslims. Not everyone who obeys Allah, practices the pillars of faith, and follows the Quran is promised eternal life. For the Muslim then, faith is all about practicing the rules to be the most diligent of Muslims.

*Leader and Revelation*

Hinduism

Hinduism has two basic texts, the Smriti (which means "that which is remembered") and the Shruti (which means "that which is revealed"). The authors of the Smriti actually record differing assertions of Hinduism, some of which are contradictory. The Shruti is supposed to be the eternal truth of Hinduism and is considered to be authorless (or of divine origin). However, Hindu scholars even disagree whether these are truly divine writings. Ultimately, these texts give guidance, but the path to truth may be different for each individual.

Buddhism

Buddhism was founded by an Indian prince named Siddhartha Gautama around the year 500 BC. According to tradition, the young prince lived an affluent and sheltered life until he made a journey where he saw an old man, a sick man, a poor man, and a corpse. Shocked and distressed at the suffering in the world, Gautama left his family to seek enlightenment through asceticism (extreme self-denial). But even the most extreme asceticism failed to bring enlightenment. Finally, Gautama sat beneath a tree and vowed not to move until he had attained enlightenment. Days later, he arose as the Buddha — the "enlightened one." He spent the remaining forty-five years of his life teaching the path to liberation from suffering (the dharma) and establishing a community of monks (the sangha). There is no holy text for Buddhists; it relies on Buddha's teachings and explanations (sutras) to be passed down by word of mouth.

Islam

In AD 610, Mohammed received his revelation from the angel Gabriel. The revelations continued for another twenty-three years and were compiled together into the Quran. From 610 to 622 Mohammed preached this revealed truth in Mecca as a peaceful religion. But in 622, he was met with hostility and persecution by the other Meccan tribes, so Mohammed and his followers fled to the nearby town of Medina living the next ten years as outcasts. During that time, the once peaceful religion of Islam turned into a religion of war and violence. Mohammed was able to change from just a religious leader to a political leader, and he sanctioned the use of violence and war to reconquer Mecca. This turn to violence can be seen in the Quran chapter 9 where unbelievers are to become "objects of the sword." In 632, Mohammed led 10,000 of his followers back to Mecca and retook the city.

The sources of authority for the Muslim come from the Quran (scriptures), the Hadith (sayings and traditions about Mohammed), and the Sharia (Islamic law). Mohammed is seen as a sinless prophet, the example for all mankind to emulate.

*Preparation of the Follower*

Hinduism

Hindus must go to great lengths to prepare their bodies for entering the temple for worship. One example is found in the Hindu festival Thaipusam celebrated in Malaysia. To prepare their bodies for entering their temple and to gain favor of their god, they use iron spears to pierce their bodies. Skewers are forced from one side of their faces through to the other. Other skewers are used to pierce their tongues. They also pierce their backs with hooks, attach ropes to them, and have someone hold the ropes to pull them in different directions. The devotees parade for hours like this while making their journey over several miles to the temple. At the end of the parade, they climb one hundred steps to the temple of the second son of the Hindu god Shiva. They then put on their forehead ashes from the burning of "purified" cow dung. Hindus go through this ceremony in order to win the blessing of the Hindu god, to respect the sanctity of the temple, and to be blessed by the priest.[14]

Buddhism

The goal for the Buddhist is to generate a positive state of mind which is achieved through meditation. A meditation session generally has three stages: preparation, meditation, and post-meditation. Lines are recited to help achieve a positive state of mind. For the new Buddhist, it is recommended to recite the four Refuge and Bodhicitta lines three times before the meditation session and the four Dedication lines after the meditation session. The important thing is to gently bring the mind to a calm and positive state before entering the meditation and afterwards to dedicate the fruits of your meditation to the benefit of others.[15]

Post-meditation refers to the time between the conclusion of this meditation session and the beginning of the next. Buddhists are advised to mark the transition from the meditation session to the post-meditation session with dedications and aspirations or prayers, as it is considered "beneficial for the development of the mind."[16]

There are several written lines to meditate on and prayers to be recited during the meditation session. However, the Buddhist chants and recitations are not exactly like praying. There is never the concept of "asking" for anything because, for the Buddhist, there is nobody to ask—there is no god. The chants are used as a meditation object, as a reminder, and as a focus for good heart, good intentions, and loving kindness. More precisely, the Buddhist is saying, "May all beings be free from suffering."[17]

Islam

Muslims follow strict rules for prayer and must cleanse themselves properly for each prayer session. They are to pray five times a day, facing toward Mecca. The summons for prayer is announced by a muezzin (caller) from atop the minaret (tall tower). Before prayer, the body must be purified by water or sand, if water is not available. The hands, feet, face, and genitals all are to be washed. Even the bathrooms are so arranged that the occupant will face in the direction of Mecca. For prayer, the Muslim bows and kneels into a prostrate position with the forehead touching the ground.[18]

Contrast with Christianity

A comparison of the doctrines of these major world religions shows that there are vast differences between them. Each of them excludes the other, making it impossible for all religions to be the same and therefore impossible for all religions to be right. If the Muslim is correct, then the Buddhist has lost his chance at salvation because he has not followed the Quran. But as different as these religions are from one another, they do have similar characteristics that set them apart from Christianity. Each of these other religions is based on the revelation provided by one man using a holy text of rules or sayings to guide the believer into a life of devotion to those rules for a salvation that is not guaranteed. Compare these religions now with the doctrine of Christianity.

Comparisons of World Religions[10]

|  | Hinduism | Buddhism | Islam | Christianity |
|---|---|---|---|---|
| Method | Yoga, meditation | Follow the Eight-Fold Path on how to end suffering | Follow the Five Pillars | Faith in Jesus |
| Goal/ Salvation | Deny reality and improve karma to reach a state where reincarnation stops—nirvana | Eliminate desire to achieve deliverance (moksha), but not sure what eternal life brings | Only the most diligent achieve eternal life | Eternal life in Heaven |
| Leader/ Revelation | None | Buddha | Mohammed | Jesus |
| Text | Smriti and Shruti | No main text; passed by word of mouth - Buddha's teachings (sutras) - Notebook for monks (Vinaya) | Quran | Bible |

*Holy Text*

The revelation of Christianity comes from forty different authors from various backgrounds across a 1500-year span that all converge to one consistent message in the Bible.[19]

*Leader / Revelation*

At the heart of every major religion, there is a leading espouser. But during the study of each religion, there becomes a dividing point or a distinction between the person and the teaching: Mohammed vs. the Koran; Buddha vs. the Noble Path; Hindu guru vs. the holy texts.

All of these teachers point to their teachings to show some particular way or path. They provide an instruction or a way of living. Meaning, it is not Mohammed who transforms you, but the Koran that guides you. It is not Buddha who delivers you, but your adherence to the Noble Truths he teaches. The uniqueness in Christianity is that Jesus did not just teach or espouse some path to follow—He was identical to His message. He didn't just proclaim truth, He WAS truth. He didn't show a way, He WAS the way.[20]

And in following that way, we are given an assurance of salvation. For the three other major world religions, there is no guarantee of salvation: Hindus just continue to try to improve their karma through reincarnation; Buddhists desire to eliminate all desire; Muslims work for their salvation which may or may not be secured even after all their devotion. Only the Christian has an assurance of the afterlife. Romans 10:13 says, "For whoever calls on the name of the Lord shall be saved." There is assurance of salvation for the Christian who calls on the name of the Lord.

*Preparation of the Follower*

We come as we are—as sinners—to Christ for forgiveness. We do not have to prepare ourselves or fix ourselves or adhere to a set of rules before we can come as disciples. It is not by the order of rules that we are cleansed. It is by the blood of Jesus Christ. We do not turn in any certain direction to pray. We are not bound by having to go to a specific building to commune with God. We don't have any specific posture or times or limitations for our access to God.[21] Other religions fight wars over the disrespect and destruction of a temple, but Christians take that temple with us wherever we go.

Every religion has its own set of rules and laws to adhere to: Quran, Eight-Fold Path, Yoga, Ten Commandments. Any religion can offer rules, but it is not by the order of the rules that we are cleansed. The law in all of these religions, including Judaism, functions like a mirror. It is there to show us how dirty our face is, but it is not there to clean our dirty faces. We wouldn't clean our face by wiping it on the mirror.[22]

The law only shows us where we fail, but it can't change us so that we can adhere perfectly to the law. *What happens when we fail to adhere strictly to the rules?* What then sets us back at right with God? In Christianity, Jesus shows us how far from the perfection of law we really are, but we can't possibly clean ourselves enough to meet the law. Therefore it takes someone perfectly observing the law, like Jesus, to be our sacrifice for it.

Any religion can point out all the rules you should follow for good behavior. But the rules themselves can't make you **righteous**. Like that mirror, it can show you that your face is dirty, but the mirror will not wash your face.

Separation from God Due to Sin

And now we can find the uniqueness in Christianity. No other religion can solve the issue of separation of us from God due to sin.

These other religions are humans trying to follow rules, or eliminate desire, or improve their karma in an effort to appease a god and achieve a blissful eternity. Yet all of these rules are human inventions. We have to ask ourselves *what it is that God demands*. God demands perfection. That Moral Law Giver who is interested in doing right, good behavior, and fair play must hate any behavior that goes against that Moral Law. In order for God to be truly good, He has to hate all evil, all violations of the Moral Law. The justice of a good and loving God must be meted out on anything that falls short of keeping that law perfectly—in deed and thought. If there were no consequences for breaking His law, then He would be unjust. He would then cease to be good. Therefore we know there must be consequences for breaking his Law.

> Just like in a human court of law, a judge that never punished or incriminated the criminal would never be considered good. He would actually be considered evil. It takes ruling in proper justice to be moral and good. Since we all have violated the Moral Law, we must all face a judgment for those offenses.

*How can we possibly keep that law perfectly?* How can the Buddhist always strictly follow the Eight-Fold Path? How can the Muslim perfectly follow the Quran? How can the Hindu ensure that there will always be a positive state of mind at death? Striving to follow those rules can't possibly erase our sin nature. Rules can't reconcile all those times where we've failed. The rules can't impart righteousness and perfection on us.

Christianity has a God that knows we cannot reach him on our own merits. So He sacrificed Himself to provide us that path. We don't have to be perfect by our own power; God provides the way for us. Only through the sacrifice of Jesus can we be made righteous by transferring our sins onto Him while He transfers

His righteousness onto us. No other religion provides a solution to our sin. No other religion can erase our debts from our immorality. God perfectly balanced His justice for punishing us for our crimes with His love for taking on that punishment in our place.

All these other religions teach that salvation is accomplished through human effort, that it is works based, earned through human strength. Only one of them teaches that man's salvation rests on the provision and grace of God. Only this religion addresses the problem of God's dual nature—absolute justice and absolute love.[23]

The moment we commit our first sin, in deed and thought, we must be eternally separated from God. God knew the only way to resolve that separation is by having the perfect sacrifice, where God could transfer our sins onto Jesus and His righteousness onto us. We can't just try to follow a bunch of rules to be in God's presence—we have to be righteous, and that is something we can't do on our own.

> "Moses could mediate the law; Muhammad could brandish a sword; Buddha could give personal counsel; Confucius could offer wise sayings, but none of these men was qualified to offer an atonement for the sins of the world ... Christ alone is worthy of unlimited devotion and service." R.C. Sproul[24]

## Truth of Christianity Excludes

If we believe that Jesus is God, then we cannot believe that any other way is true.

The statement made by Jesus that He is the way, the truth, and the life is a truth claim. He is saying first that truth is **absolute,** and second that truth is **knowable.** His claim is that anything that contradicts that is by definition false.[25] It is therefore exclusive.

If you have become a Christian and accepted that God sent His one and only Son to die for your sins, then any other pathway to eternal salvation cannot be true. By accepting Jesus as your Savior, you accept that He is perfect and holy. Therefore, He cannot lie. That means His statement that no man comes to the Father except through Him is truth. Therefore, no man can come to the Father through Islam, through Buddhism, through Hinduism, through atheism, through sincerity of belief, or through ignorance.

Jesus did not die as a martyr for a cause; nor was He just nonviolent so that the enemy would surrender through public outcry. He came to lay down His life so that the very ones who killed Him—who represented all of us—could be forgiven.[26] By allowing any other way to Heaven besides through Jesus, we cheapen the sacrifice He made and we call Jesus a liar. Simply put, if there were any other way to gain salvation, why would He have gone through the suffering and death that he went through?

The resurrection of Jesus established Him as being the Son of God. Because that is true, then all other faith systems cannot be true because they assert something contrary to his divinity. But even better, because the resurrection is real, we can be forgiven, we can be reconciled with God, we can spend eternity with Him, and we can trust Jesus' teachings as being from God.[27]

So why do people not choose Christianity?

Because Christianity demands a commitment from you. Buddhism sounds good because you can be good without having God. You have no accountability to anyone but yourself. Islam sounds good because of geopolitical reasons. Hinduism sounds good because it has a rich philosophy and respect for the earth. All of these pull on some popular ideology in our culture today. But Christianity requires you to die to yourself. And anytime truth involves a total commitment in which you bring yourself to complete humility, to the surrender of your will, you will always have resistance to it.[28]

*What about the people in the village in Africa that have never heard of Jesus?* They will still be lost and condemned to hell because they do not have saving faith in Jesus Christ.

If we allow people to be saved simply because they haven't heard, then we have again diminished the sacrifice of Jesus and have called him a liar. We have in effect declared that there is in fact another way to the Father—through ignorance.

If we allow those to be saved just because they haven't heard, then we should stop witnessing! It would be only after they hear and reject the word of God that they would be condemned. But Jesus didn't tell us to believe in Him and be quiet about it in case someone hasn't heard. Jesus told us to go and tell others. He commanded that because that is the only way others can be saved.

As far as never hearing the name of Jesus, God does judge us according to how much has been revealed to us. But there is still the necessity of faith in Jesus Christ for salvation.

Luke 12:47–48 And that servant who knew his master's will, and did not prepare himself or do according to his will, shall be beaten with many stripes. But he who did not know, yet committed things deserving of stripes, shall be beaten with few. For everyone to whom much is given, from him much will be required; and to whom much has been committed, of him they will ask the more.

Notice both disobedient servants are beaten, but the one who did not know is not beaten as much. In other words, those without Jesus will still be condemned. Those who have heard Jesus and rejected Him will be punished worse than those who never heard at all.

*How do we reconcile a loving God with one who condemns people for never hearing about Jesus?* We have to balance God's justice with God's Sovereignty.

God knows the heart and will provide a way for those who sincerely seek Him.[29] God provides a way for them to learn about Jesus—either through a missionary, finding a Bible, hearing a radio broadcast, or even in visions and dreams. This should show us the importance of our obedience when God calls us to be that missionary.

We see this in action in Acts 19. Paul encounters some disciples in Ephesus who knew of the teachings of John the Baptist but had not learned fully the teaching of Jesus. Paul is able to tell that their knowledge stops short because they don't know of the indwelling of the Holy Spirit.

As sincere as those disciples were, and as dedicated to the partial truth from God, they did not have saving faith because they did not have a full knowledge of Jesus, nor did they have the indwelling of the Holy Spirit. Sad though it is to think, these disciples were not saved just like anyone whose knowledge may stop short of the full truth of Jesus.

People without Jesus are not saved even though they may be sincere or may be close to the truth. This is why it is so critical to not pervert or twist any portion of the scripture. Any teaching that alters the scripture could result in a person not having full saving faith.

In His Sovereignty, God sent Paul to the disciples in Ephesus at just the right time for their hearts to be brought into the full knowledge and full saving faith in Jesus. In His Sovereignty, God sent Philip to the Ethiopian eunuch while he was reading from Isaiah (Acts 8). God sent Peter to Cornelius because he was faithful (Acts 10). God sent Priscilla and Aquila to Apollos because he was fervent to teach others (Acts 18).

These aren't just lucky coincidences for these people—these are God-directed interventions to provide salvation for those who are seeking truth. For those who are searching, even if it is in a remote African village, God will provide a way for them to learn about Jesus.

Conclusion

Despite the popular platitudes about religion, not all religions are the same. They each have vastly different doctrines when it comes to defining who saves us, what the afterlife is, and how we get there. In looking at three major worldviews, we can see each of them provides a different response to those questions. However, a common theme does emerge—they all involve man's efforts based on man's standard. Mohammed offers the Muslims the codes within the Quran. Buddha offers the endless rules of the Eight-Fold Path. The Hindu relies on the diligent practice of yoga and meditation. Each method is designed to confine man's behavior to meet some acceptable standard that man has defined. But none of them consider what the standard set by God actually is. And none of these actually provide a solution for when that standard is violated. None of them can actually fix mankind from their wrongdoings.

Christianity is unique in that it is a solution provided by God based on God's standard. God knows that we can't perfectly adhere to the law, so He provided a way to give us the righteousness that is required. Because we know God gave us the Moral Law to compel us to right behavior, we know that God is good and interested in our being good. In order to remain good, God must judge our bad behavior, otherwise He ceases to be good. Since rules and rituals established by man cannot erase our bad behavior, God had to provide another way for reconciliation. He provided that path through the perfect sacrifice of Jesus Christ.

## QUESTIONS FOR CONSIDERATION

Why can't all religions be the same? What law of logic is violated by saying all religions are true?

Does the fact that people believe so many things make those things true?

If religions seem similar, what is it that makes them different?

What sets Jesus apart from other religious leaders?

What distinguishes Christianity from other religions?

What purpose do religious rules serve? Can those rules make us righteous?

How can man solve the issue of our separation from God due to sin?

If Christianity is true, can other ways to heaven be valid?

Can people be saved simply because they've never heard of Jesus?

How do we have confidence that God will provide a way of salvation to those who seek Him?

# WHO WAS JESUS?

1 John 1:3 That which we have seen and heard we declare to you, that you also may have fellowship with us; and truly our fellowship is with the Father and with His Son Jesus Christ.

Mark 8:29 Jesus said to them, "But who do you say that I am?"

# LESSON 5

## Validity of the New Testament

### INTRODUCTION

The first three lessons have confirmed there is a God. From cause and effect, there must be a cause that resulted in the effect of the universe. From the design within the universe and within our cells, we know there must be a designer. Because we have a spirit and morality, we know that something spiritual and moral must have given those things to us. So we know that there is a God that caused us, designed us, gave us a spirit, and imparted a sense of morality. In the last lesson we took a deeper look at what god must be responsible for that. Because of the Law of Non-contradiction, all religions cannot be true. Since they all contradict each other, only one of them can be right. We saw that the Christian God is truly unique from other world religions. All other religions offer rules to follow, but those rules can't make us righteous. The rules can't solve the issue of our sin nature. But the truths about the

Christian God and the reconciliation of our sin depend on the truth about Jesus as the Son of God. So now we must investigate who Jesus really was.

## STUDY

To investigate the life of Jesus, we must turn to the most extensive recorded accounts of his life—the New Testament. The truth of the Christian faith depends on the historical nature and accuracy of the unique claims made about the character and credentials of Jesus Christ found in the Gospel writings. The claims of Christianity can only be true if these writings convey factually reliable information. If, however, the Gospels contain mythical or legendary accounts of Jesus Christ, then the truth claims contained therein cannot be trusted. In other words, there is no point in discussing the ramifications of the life of anyone if it turns out their biography was just a work of fiction. We need to determine if the account of Jesus' life in the Bible is accurate and trustworthy. In order to assess the credentials of the New Testament, we will use the same three criteria that would be used to judge any work from antiquity[1]:

1. Bibliographical test: that the text we have now is what was originally recorded.
2. Internal evidence test: that the text is credible.
3. External evidence test: that other historical texts confirm the contents.

Bibliographical Test

*Dating of the New Testament*

Many critics question the historical accuracy of the Bible by questioning the dates in which it was written. Most of them insist the New Testament was written several centuries after

Jesus, implying the Gospel accounts are the result of the game of "telephone." The assertion is that so much time had passed between the events and the Gospel writings that things were taken out of context, stretched into a legend, or misinterpreted as the information was handed down over generations.

The first thing to establish then is the proximity of the original authors to the events they recorded, both in time and place. In other words, a document you write about the events in your town from this past year would be more reliable than your account of the French Revolution ... because you are in your town during this past year and not in France in the late 1700s. When we look closely at the New Testament authors, we find that they are writing firsthand accounts of events they had witnessed. This proximity of the authors to these events is an effective means to certify the accuracy of what was recorded.

Let's start with the archeological discoveries dated most recently and work backwards through time to the life and ministry of Jesus Christ, circa AD 30.[2]

1.  Fragments of the Gospel of John were found in Egypt dating from the early second century, between AD 100 and 150. At most, the Gospel of John was written 120 years after the life, death, and resurrection of Jesus. And it was already in circulation as far away as Egypt.[3]

2.  New Testament gospels are cited in other first-century works (up to AD 100) such as *The Epistle of Barnabas*, *The Didache*, Clement's *Corinthians*, and Ignatius's *Seven Epistles*. This indicates the New Testament gospels were already well-established in order to be referenced in other works.[4]

3.  Based on the archaeological discovery of second century papyri documents and the comparison of the Greek language between those and the New Testament, historians

agree that the New Testament manuscripts had to have been written **between AD 50 and 75**, none of them being written later than AD 80.[5]

4. The book of Acts is dated to circa AD 62, definitely no later than AD 64. This date has been determined by several factors, one being the information that is not included in the text. Luke, the author, was very meticulous about providing detailed information. He lists specific names of towns, rulers, governors, and members of the priesthood for when certain events take place. He is so specific that he is considered a first-class historian for his accounts in both the Book of Acts and the Gospel of Luke.[6] However, he concludes Acts during the first imprisonment of Paul in Rome (AD 62). Had Luke been writing this later than that, he most likely would have included such events as the:
   - Fall of Jerusalem under Titus (AD 70)
   - Persecution by Nero (mid-60s)
   - Martyrdom of the three major early church leaders:
     - James, Jesus' brother and the leader of the Jerusalem church (AD 62)
     - Peter and Paul (AD 67 or 68)

Each of these events had a major impact on Christianity and would certainly be included in discussing the life and times of the early church formation. But Luke does not include any of those major events affecting Christianity within the Book of Acts. It indicates he wrote Acts before those events took place.[7]

5. Acts was also written as the sequel to the Gospel of Luke. Both are written to Theophilus and in the introduction to the Book of Acts, Luke references his "former account" of the Gospel of Luke. Therefore, with Acts being written

no later than AD 62, then the Gospel of Luke was written several years earlier.[8]

6. It is estimated that Matthew was written within twenty years of Jesus' death and resurrection, which would be around AD 53.[9]

   ▪ Bishop John A.T. Robinson states in *Redating the New Testament* that all of the New Testament was written prior to AD 70, before the fall of Jerusalem. More specifically, he concludes that all of the New Testament was written between AD 40 and 63.[10]

7. It has been estimated that Paul wrote 1 Corinthians in about AD 55 or 56 based on his missionary journey timeline.[11] Paul was beheaded in Rome by Nero in AD 64 so that is the latest possible date. The date for 1 Corinthians is only about twenty-two years after Jesus' death and resurrection, and while most of the 500 witnesses of Jesus' resurrection were still alive. In Paul's letter to the church in Corinth, he tells about the death and resurrection of Jesus.

*"For I delivered to you first of all that which I also received: that Christ died for our sins according to the Scriptures, and that He was buried, and that He rose again the third day according to the Scriptures, and that He was seen by Cephas, then by the twelve. After that He was seen by over five hundred brethren at once, of whom the greater part remain to the present, but some have fallen asleep. After that He was seen by James, then by all the apostles. Then last of all He was seen by me also, as by one born out of due time."* 1 Corinthians 15:3–8

Dating the crucifixion of Jesus at AD 30, we can estimate Paul's conversion on the road to Damascus to be circa AD 32. Paul preached there in Damascus for a time, but then he left for Jerusalem somewhere around AD 35 and met some of the disciples. During his time either in Jerusalem or while being mentored in Damascus, Paul had been taught basic doctrinal facts about Jesus' life, death, and resurrection, which he then records in 1 Corinthians 15. Those key facts are that Jesus died for our sins, He was buried and resurrected, and His resurrection was witnessed by specific individuals as well as a multitude of people. Paul had been taught those things within two to five years of their occurrence. Paul had then been preaching those facts to others and makes reference of that in a letter to the church in Corinth within twenty years of those same events.[12] By Paul recording those details in his letter in AD 56, he confirms that those teachings of the life, death, resurrection, and miracles of Jesus were being taught well before AD 56, which is an extremely small gap in time between the events and their first documentation.

We know that Jesus' death under Pilate occurred between AD 30 and 33. Because the Gospels of Mark and Luke were written no later than AD 62, those books are within thirty years of Jesus' life, death, and resurrection, or basically within one generation. Given the early dates from Bishop Robinson, some of the Gospels were written within only seven years of those events.

We must conclude then that the New Testament was written so close in time to the events they report that it would not have allowed enough time for myths to have developed. This is especially true since many of the eyewitnesses were still alive to correct any misreporting. There simply wasn't enough time between the events of the New Testament and the writings of the New Testament to allow for myth and legend to grow about Jesus.

*Manuscript Evidence*

Another method used to assess the historical accuracy of a document when we don't have the original is to look at the manuscript evidence. This method evaluates the number of

**manuscripts (a handwritten copy)** and the time interval between the manuscript and the original **(the autograph)**. The shorter the time period between the autograph and the date of its first manuscript, the more reliable a text is considered to be. A short time period means there is less time for the document to be corrupted through transmission or interpolation.[13]

For most ancient classics, very few manuscripts actually exist (consider the works of Aristotle, Plato, Caesar, Tacitus, Thucydides, Herodotus, etc.). The best cases average about twenty extant manuscripts for any given historical work. There is also an average gap of over 1,000 years between the original work (autograph) and the date of its earliest existing copy (manuscript).[14]

- History of Thucydides who lived from 460–400 BC is found in only eight manuscripts dating around AD 900 (nearly 1300 year gap).[15]
- Aristotle's documents were written in 343 BC, but the earliest manuscript we have is from AD 1100, and there are only five manuscripts (nearly 1500-year gap).[16]
- Caesar's composition about the Gallic Wars was written between 58 and 50 BC, and there are only ten manuscripts dated from about AD 950 (just over 1,000-year gap).[17]
- *Annals of Imperial Rome* was written by Tacitus in AD 116. The first six books have only one manuscript dating from AD 850; books eleven through sixteen are in another manuscript from the eleventh century; books seven through ten have been lost completely (best case is a 700-year gap).[18]
- *The Jewish War* was written by Josephus in the first century. There are only nine Greek manuscripts that were written in the tenth, eleventh, and twelfth centuries (roughly 900-year gap).[19]

- Homer's *Iliad* was written in 800 BC; we have 650 Greek manuscripts from the second and third century AD (over 1,000-year gap).[20]

Even with those large time gaps and scant manuscript texts, none of those ancient works are rejected as inauthentic or unreliable by the accepted standards of historiography. The reality is that some ancient documents are accepted as authentic texts with extremely thin manuscript attestation.[21]

Now let's look at the manuscript evidence for the New Testament books.

- More than 5,000 individual Greek manuscripts that contain all or part of the New Testament have been found. These manuscripts are augmented by more than 10,000 copies of the Vulgate (an important Latin version of the Bible translated by the early fifth-century Western church father Jerome).[22]
- In total, the New Testament has 24,970 manuscripts all within 350 years of the events they relate, the earliest of them dating to AD 50–60.[23]
- The oldest copy of any portion of the New Testament in existence today is the John Rylands' manuscript. It is a papyrus fragment that contains just a few verses from the Gospel of John (John 18:31–33, 37–38). It was discovered in Egypt and has been dated circa AD 117–138. Assuming John's Gospel was written between AD 60 and AD 90, the time gap amounts to only several decades at most. This is far superior to any other accepted classical literature.[24]
- The Bodmer Papyri contains part of the New Testament Gospels (including most of the Gospels of Luke and John) and dates to AD 200.[25]

- The Beatty Papyri contains almost all of the New Testament (including large portions of all four Gospels) and dates to AD 250. Bodmer and Beatty are then roughly 100 to 200 years removed. By textual standards, this time frame is incredibly brief for ancient writings.[26]
- There are five important Greek uncial writings. These are written in a special type of capital letters, on parchment (scraped animal skin) instead of papyrus, and in codex form (arranged more like a modern book) instead of in scroll form.[27]

  - Codex Sinaiticus - Contains entire New Testament and parts of the Old Testament. Dates from AD 340.
  - Codex Vaticanus - Includes almost the entire Bible. Dates from AD 325–350.
  - Codex Alexandrinus - Contains most of the Bible. Dates from AD 450.
  - Codex Bezae - Written in Greek and Latin, includes parts of the New Testament (most of the four Gospels). Dates circa AD 450–550.
  - Codex Ephraemi - Contains part of the Old Testament and most of the New Testament. Dates from AD 400.

In addition to the manuscripts of the Gospel text itself, there are thousands of specific scriptural references and citations that have been preserved in sermons, commentaries, and other works of the early church fathers, from the second through the fifth centuries. This gives further confirmation of the early dates in which the Gospels were originally written and distributed if they were being quoted by the second century.

The New Testament shows immense superiority to all other classical works of antiquity in terms of the time between the autographs and the earliest existing copies.

*"The interval then between the dates of the original composition and the earliest extant evidence becomes so small as to be in fact negligible, and the last foundation for any doubt that the Scriptures have come down to us substantially as they were written has now been removed. Both the authenticity and general integrity of the books of the New Testament may be regarded as finally established."* Sir Frederic Kenyon, an expert on ancient manuscripts[28]

*"To be skeptical of the resultant text of the New Testament books is to allow all of classical antiquity to slip into obscurity, for no documents of the ancient period are as well attested bibliographically as the New Testament."* John Warwick Montgomery, *History and Christianity*[29]

*Reliability of the Copies*

We've established the New Testament books were written within the same generation as the events they describe (some estimates say as early as seven years later). And we've demonstrated there is more manuscript evidence to show the validity of the New Testament books than any other accepted ancient literature. However, *what if those documents have been altered through the course of time to become what we know as our Bible today?*

For years our oldest manuscripts of the Old Testament came from the 10th century AD (these were known as the Masoretic text). Many people claimed that because these were so far after the events they reported, that surely something was written down wrong or over time things had been subtracted from or added to the text. But in the 1940s the Dead Sea Scrolls were discovered, estimated circa 300 BC. Experts could now compare what was captured in each set of documents to see how much of the text had been changed over time.

After careful analysis it was discovered there was an unbelievable amount of accuracy between the Masoretic text and the Dead Sea Scrolls. For example, the copies of Isaiah in the Dead Sea Scrolls are virtual matches to the Masoretic text. The text from the Old Testament had remained stable for more than a thousand years and now there is the evidence to prove it.[30]

Biblical scribes were meticulous with an unusual level of accuracy in how they copied Scripture. The reliability of those copies has been measured by reconstructing the original text from the manuscripts that we possess. Although a few copyist errors had been found, the original text was copied to what we have today with more than 95 percent accuracy. The remaining 5 percent can be attributed to simple slips of the pen or changing of spelling.

*As Millar Burrows states: "Of the 166 words in Isaiah 53, there are only seventeen **letters** in question. Ten of these letters are simply a matter of spelling ... four more letters are minor stylistic changes, such as conjunctions.... The remaining three letters comprise the word "light" in verse 11 ... and does not affect the meaning greatly.... It is a matter of wonder that through something like a thousand years the text underwent so little alteration."*[31]

In places where errors were found, they were in minor areas, things that have no doctrinal impact. The transcription errors were in things like the number of horse stalls Solomon had or the age of Ahaziah when he was king. In fact, even for these copyist errors it's actually quite easy to determine which number is correct based on the context of the surrounding text. The findings of the Dead Sea Scrolls proved that every important truth of Scripture had remained intact and preserved for the thousands of years that it had been transcribed.

*What about all the different translations we have today?*

Reputable versions start with the oldest and best Greek manuscripts (New Testament) and Hebrew manuscripts (Old Testament) that we possess, and these are then translated directly into the contemporary language. So other translations done in the interim mean nothing to the question of accuracy because today's Bibles go back to the original ancient texts, not intermediary translations.[32]

*What about "gospel" books that were left out of the Bible?* Maybe those were telling a different side to Jesus that the Church left out so as not to taint their religion.

Those books actually weren't included for the reason that they were written so much later than the events—well into the second and fourth centuries. They were not accounts from an eyewitness. None of them have apostolic authority, or ties back to the apostles. This point goes to testify how diligent they were about what *should* be included in the Bible since those later books were excluded.[33]

One way to confirm that is the different level of detail between the Gospels and the books written much later. The Gospels mention numerous small villages and towns that affirm the writers were from those areas and familiar with the landscape and geography. The later books only include the larger city names, making no mention of the smaller towns. It was as though they were written by people from another time and place with no familiarity of those details. For that very reason, those books have been excluded. They are more likely to contain falsities and mistakes because of the length of time between when the events occurred and the authors. This speaks volumes to the integrity of what is contained in the New Testament. Only documents written by those who were directly involved in the events recorded were included in the New Testament.

The bibliography of the New Testament assures us that it actually has more manuscript authority than any other piece of literature from antiquity that is otherwise accepted. The authenticity of the New Testament has been well established.[34]

Internal Evidence Test

The bibliography of the New Testament only assures us that the words we have now are the words that were initially recorded. But what about the authors themselves? Were they conspiring to invent their own new religion? Can we trust that the original words were true?

*Credibility of the Authors*

The credibility of the authors can be established in the following ways:

1. The Gospels were written either by an eyewitness or directly from an eyewitness.[35]
   - 2 Peter 1:16 "For we did not follow cunningly devised fables when we made known to you the power and coming of our Lord Jesus Christ, but **were eyewitnesses** of His majesty." (written by Peter)
   - Acts 2:32 "This Jesus God has raised up, of which **we are all witnesses**." (spoken by Peter)
   - Acts 10:39 "And **we are witnesses** of all things which He did both in the land of the Jews and in Jerusalem, whom they killed by hanging on a tree." (spoken by Peter)

- 1 John 1:3 "That which **we have seen and heard** we declare to you, that you also may have fellowship with us; and truly our fellowship is with the Father and with His Son Jesus Christ." (written by John)
- John 19:35 "And he who has seen has testified, and his testimony is true; and he knows that he is telling the truth, so that you may believe." (written by John)
- Matthew 10:18 "You will be brought before governors and kings for My sake, as **a testimony** to them and to the Gentiles." (spoken by Jesus to the disciples)
- Luke 1:1–3 (NIV) "With this in mind, **since I myself have carefully investigated everything** from the beginning, I too decided to write an orderly account for you, most excellent Theophilus." (written by Luke)

2. The New Testament authors appealed to others as eyewitnesses, even those who did not believe

- Acts 2:22–23 "Men of Israel, hear these words: Jesus of Nazareth, a Man attested by God to you by miracles, wonders, and signs which God did through Him in your midst, as you yourselves also know—Him, being delivered by the determined purpose and foreknowledge of God, you have taken by lawless hands, have crucified, and put to death."
- Acts 26:26 "For the king, before whom I also speak freely, knows these things; for I am convinced that none of these things escapes his attention, since this thing was not done in a corner."

3. The disciples were writing these things at the same time as witnesses who were critics, so they could not afford to have inaccuracies in their accounts. In fact, the New Testament writers were actively working to squelch rumors and

untruths before they started. Paul was continually writing to warn his churches of following after false doctrine.

*Lawrence J. McGinley of St. Peter's College says, "First of all, eyewitnesses of the events in question were still alive when the tradition had been completely formed; and among those eyewitnesses were bitter enemies of the new religious movement. Yet the tradition claimed to narrate a series of well-known deeds and publicly taught doctrines at a time when false statements could, and would, be challenged."*[36]

4. They were selective about what was considered canon for the New Testament. They only allowed the writings of those who came from someone in the apostolic circles and included eyewitnesses or associates of eyewitnesses. We know they held to that standard in their writings because of what has been excluded today. We see that same standard being applied when the disciples were setting the criteria to replace the disciple Judas (ref. Acts 1:21–22). The new apostle had to have been there from the beginning. He had to have witnessed the life and ministry of Jesus, from His baptism to His death, His resurrection, and His ascension in order to be considered one of the twelve. They made that criteria so that the full apostolic authority could be maintained.

The writers for both Testaments were by and large contemporaries of the events they were writing about. This adds to their credibility in the same way that your book on the happenings in your town from this year is more credible than your book on the French Revolution. You have more credibility in the former because you are living in that place and time. This holds true for the Old Testament writings as well. Moses was a witness of the events recorded in Exodus through Deuteronomy,

Joshua was for his book, as were Samuel, Isaiah, Jeremiah, Daniel, Ezra, Nehemiah, and many others. Let's take a look at each of the New Testament books and their authors.

<u>Gospel of Matthew:</u> Manuscript evidence and early church acceptance confirms that the Gospel of Matthew was written by Matthew, one of the disciples of Jesus. There are also early manuscript copies with Matthew's name attached to it that were circulated around AD 125. During the years of the early church, his authorship was never disputed.[37] Therefore, this is a firsthand account of the life and ministry of Jesus by a disciple who had been there for everything.

<u>Gospel of Mark:</u> The Gospel of Mark was written by John Mark, cousin of Barnabas and associate of the apostle Paul. Though Mark was not one of the twelve, Mark's gospel actually reflects the eyewitness testimony of the apostle Peter. Mark took the basic preached message of Peter and arranged and shaped that message into the Gospel of Mark. New Testament scholar, F.F. Bruce states, "Mark's use of pronouns in narratives involving Peter seems time after time to reflect a reminiscence by that apostle in the first person."[38]

<u>Gospel of John:</u> The Gospel of John was written by John, one of the disciples of Jesus. John gives detailed knowledge of first-century Jewish culture, custom, and theology, as well as a keen awareness of the geography of ancient Israel. He refers to himself as the disciple "whom Jesus loved." From John we not only get a firsthand account of the life, ministry, death, and resurrection of Jesus from a disciple, but from Jesus' closest friend, the one whom Jesus entrusts to care for His mother. He was there at Jesus' transfiguration, last supper, crucifixion, and saw the resurrected Jesus firsthand.[39] He confirms his authorship at the end of his Gospel:

John 21:24–25 *"This is the disciple who testifies of these things, and wrote these things; and we know that his testimony is true. And there are also many other things that Jesus did, which if they were written one by one, I supposed that even the world itself could not contain the books that would be written. Amen."*

John again asserts his eyewitness testimony in his epistle, describing that he had personally heard, seen, and touched Jesus so he has authority to write on such things.

1 John 1:1–4 *"That which was from the beginning, which we have heard, which we have seen with our eyes, which we have looked upon, and our hands have handled, concerning the Word of life—the life was manifested, and we have seen, and bear witness, and declare to you that eternal life which was with the Father and was manifested to us—that which we have seen and heard we declare to you, that you also may have fellowship with us; and truly our fellowship is with the Father and with His Son Jesus Christ. And these things we write to you that your joy may be full."*

Gospel of Luke: The Gospel of Luke was written by Luke, a companion of the apostle Paul. While Luke was not one of the disciples himself, Luke had access to all the principle apostolic figures, including Peter and James (the brother of Jesus).

Luke 1:1–4 *"Inasmuch as many have taken in hand to set in order a narrative of those things which have been fulfilled among us, just as those who from the beginning were eyewitnesses and ministers of the word delivered them to us, it seemed good to me also, having had perfect understanding of all things from the very first, to write to you an orderly account, most excellent Theophilus, that you may know the certainty of those things in which you were instructed."*

Luke says that "many" have written an account of the life of Jesus so he decides to do so as well. That means in all likelihood, at least one of the Gospels was already in existence at this point. Although Luke was probably not a personal eyewitness to Jesus and His ministry, he sought out those who were as part of his careful investigation. If you wanted to get a detailed, true account of what happened in the Battle of the Bulge in WWII, you would search out people who fought there to get their testimony. That's exactly what Luke did. He wasn't there himself, so he looked for those who were to get their account. And he tells us why he went to such great lengths: to provide an orderly account for Theophilus. Luke wanted to make sure he got all of the facts together and in their proper order so that he could relate this account of the amazing life, death, and resurrection of Jesus to his friend Theophilus so that he would know the truth.

Luke is also considered a first-rate historian as a result of his careful investigation. From the detail that Luke provides (names, dates, events, places), historians are able to verify many of his Gospel's sources and claims. Consider the level of detail given just in the third chapter of Luke:

> Luke 3:1–2 *"Now in the fifteenth year of the reign of Tiberius Caesar, Pontius Pilate being governor of Judea, Herod tetrarch of Galilee, his brother Philip tetrarch of Iturea and the region of Trachonitis, and Lysanias tetrarch of Abilene, while Annas and Caiaphas were high priests, the word of God came to John son of Zacharias in the wilderness."*

Acts of the Apostles: Luke is also the author of the book of Acts. Though this is not one of the Gospels, it does record the ascension of Jesus, the arrival of the Holy Spirit, and the amazing growth and spread of the church. Luke does become an eyewitness of things within this book as we find the "we" passages, parts written in first person because Luke was present at the time of that event. That was when Luke was traveling with Paul on his missions. Much of the rest of the book is written in third person, but in those parts Luke is documenting what Paul was relating as the firsthand eyewitness.

Sir William Ramsay is a leading archaeologist whose work has largely been the reason the critical views of the New Testament have been overthrown and its historicity reestablished. He was converted himself from the work of Luke in the Book of Acts:

> *"I began with a mind unfavorable to it [Acts], for the ingenuity and apparent completeness of the Tubingen theory [that Acts had been written late in the second century] had at one time quite convinced me. It did not lie then in my line of life to investigate the subject minutely; but more recently I found myself often brought into contact with the book of Acts as an authority for the topography, antiquities, and society of Asia Minor. It was gradually borne in upon me that in various details the narrative showed marvelous truth."*[40]

Classical historian A.N. Sherwin-White writes, "For Acts the confirmation of historicity is overwhelming … any attempt to reject its basic historicity even in matters of detail must now appear absurd."[41]

Epistles of Peter: Although Peter didn't pen one of the Gospels himself (his account is written by Mark), we do have his letters. In his epistles, Peter affirms his eyewitness testimony and thus his authority to write on such things. He speaks out about the veracity of the Gospel truth because he had seen it and heard it himself. He was not following just rumors of something imagined, but true events that he saw and participated in.

2 Peter 1:15–18 *"Moreover, I will be careful to ensure that you always have a reminder of these things after my decease. For we did not follow cunningly devised fables when we made known to you the power and coming of our Lord Jesus Christ, but were eyewitnesses of His majesty. For He received from God the Father honor and glory when such a voice came to him from the Excellent Glory: 'This is My beloved Son, in whom I am well pleased.' And we heard this voice which came from heaven when we were with Him on the holy mountain."*

Because each of these books has apostolic association—the author had either been with Jesus or had gotten information directly from those who had—they were considered to be part of the canon. It is this eyewitness testimony that gives these authors and their writings credibility.

But there are also external ways we can attest to their credibility.

1. <u>The inclusion of material that is not flattering to themselves</u>. They included the truth about themselves and Jesus' ministry instead of only the things that portrayed them in a good light. It lends to their credibility.[42]
   - the competition of the apostles for high places in the Kingdom,
   - Jesus saying to Peter, "Get behind Me, Satan,"
   - Peter cutting off the soldier's ear at Jesus' arrest
   - their flight after Jesus' arrest,
   - Peter's denial,
   - the refusal of Christ to work miracles in Nazareth (Mark 6:5) which appears to limit Jesus' power,
   - Jesus' admission of not knowing the hour of His return (Mark 13:32) which appears to limit His omniscience, and
   - Jesus' despairing cry on the cross (Matthew 27:46).

2. <u>Their tendency to doubt whether Jesus rose from the dead</u>. The resurrection is the critical point to the Gospel, yet the authors of the New Testament admitted that they were not expecting that to happen. It showed they, too, did not have confidence in exactly who Jesus was and what was going to happen until after they saw it for themselves.
   - Matthew 28:17 When they saw Him, they worshiped Him; but some doubted.
   - Mark 16:3 And they said among themselves, "Who will roll away the stone from the door of the tomb for us?" (as they were walking to Jesus' tomb)
   - Luke 24:11 And their words seemed to them like idle tales, and they did not believe them. (The disciples did not believe the women who said the tomb was empty.)
   - John 20:24-29 doubting Thomas wanting to touch the wounds of Christ to believe it was really Him raised from the dead

3. <u>The inclusion of "hard sayings" of Jesus.</u>[43] If man were inventing a religion, he probably wouldn't tell people to be as perfect as the Heavenly Father and then define imperfection as the sin in our hearts and thoughts.
   - Jesus defined adultery as lust within the heart (Matthew 5:27–28).

4. <u>The divergence of accounts that shows they were not in collusion</u>. If the Gospels had been identical to each other, word for word, then it would appear that the authors were colluding. It would increase the likelihood that the accounts were fabrications and not independent eyewitness testimonies. However, the Gospel accounts are not carbon copies of each other. They have enough differences to be a recollection from a different observer from his personal vantage point and perspective.[44] It is comparable to you

and three friends each writing an account of the same event you all experienced. There would be four different essays that varied on certain details but agreed on the overall content.

- The Gospel of John differs enough in theme and style that it is not considered with Matthew, Mark, and Luke as a synoptic gospel.
- The differing accounts in Matthew 8:5–13 and Luke 7:1–10 of Jesus healing a centurion's servant.
- The different description of the appearance of the angel to Mary at the tomb when Jesus resurrected (ref. Matthew 28:5 and John 20:12)

5. Their willingness to die for their written accounts. All of the New Testament writers were willing to die for the claims made in their writings, and most of them did. Even more telling, they all died alone. Matthew, Mark, Luke, John, Paul, James, Peter, and Jude all died for upholding the cause of Christ in their testimonies. What this tells us is that they had very little to gain and everything to lose from the facts they were relating.[45]

- They knew the stakes were high for writing down such things but were willing to do it anyway because they knew it was the truth.
- Creating this story about Jesus as a hoax only brought them meaningless hardship, persecution, and death.
- A conspiracy to lie about these things would have fallen apart under that kind of widespread, intense persecution.
- They had no discernible motive or reason to lie about the life of Jesus. He was not the conquering Messiah the Jews were anticipating, and it only brought them suffering.

External Evidence Test

The third test in assessing the historical accuracy of a document is the external evidence test. This determines whether other historical materials outside the document confirm or deny the internal testimony of the document. *Are there other sources that can substantiate the claims made within the New Testament accounts?*

*Confirmation from Non-Biblical Sources*

The historian Eusebius preserves the writings of Papias, a bishop of Hierapolis in AD 130. These writings give confirmation of the authorship and account found in the Gospel of Mark.

> *"The Elder (Apostle John) used to say this also: 'Mark, having been the interpreter of Peter, wrote down accurately all that he [Peter] mentioned, whether sayings or doings of Christ, not, however, in order. For he was neither a hearer nor a companion of the Lord; but afterwards, as I said, he accompanied Peter, who adapted his teachings as necessity required, not as though he were making a compilation of the sayings of the Lord. So then Mark made no mistake, writing down in this way some things as he mentioned them; for he paid attention to this one thing, not to omit anything that he had heard, not to include any false statement among them.'"* [46]

Irenaeus, Bishop of Lyons in AD 180, gave further detail for the authorship of each Gospel.

> *"Matthew published his Gospel among the Hebrews in their own tongue, when Peter and Paul were preaching the gospel in Rome and founding the church there. After their departure, Mark, the disciple and interpreter of Peter, himself handed down to us in writing the substance of Peter's preaching. Luke, the follower of Paul, set down in a book the gospel preached by his teacher. Then*

*John, the disciple of the Lord ... produced his Gospel, while he was living at Ephesus in Asia."*[47]

The Jewish historian Josephus (AD 37–100) abounds with references to New Testament people and events, giving confirmation of the accuracy of the New Testament. F.F. Bruce summarized the evidence from Josephus as:

*"Here, in the pages of Josephus, we meet many figures who are well-known to us from the New Testament; the colorful family of the Herods; the Roman emperors Augustus, Tiberius, Claudius, and the procurators of Judea; the high priestly families — Annas, Caiaphas, Ananias, and the rest; the Pharisees and the Sadducees; and so on."*[48]

Josephus also wrote of "the brother of Jesus, the so-called Christ, whose name was James." And in a more explicit but disputed passage he says:

*"At this time there was a wise man who was called Jesus ... Pilate condemned Him to be condemned and to die. And those who had become His disciples did not abandon His discipleship. They reported that He had appeared to them three days after His crucifixion and that He was alive; accordingly, He was perhaps the Messiah concerning whom the prophets have recounted wonders."*[49]

There are references to Jesus Christ from Tacitus, a Roman historian from AD 56 to 117, in his account of Nero's blaming the Christians for burning Rome:

*"Nero fastened the guilt and inflicted the most exquisite tortures on a class hated for their abominations, called Christians by the populace. Christus, from whom the name had its origin,*

*suffered the extreme penalty during the reign of Tiberius at the hands of one of our procurators, Pontius Pilatus, and a most mischievous superstition, thus checked for the moment, again broke out not only in Judea, the first source of the evil, but even in Rome.... Accordingly, an arrest was first made of all who pleaded guilty: then, upon their information, an immense multitude was convicted, not so much of the crime of firing the city, as of hatred against mankind."*[50]

This gives testimony by an unsympathetic witness to the success and spread of Christianity which was based on a historical figure, Jesus Christ, crucified under Pontius Pilate. The use of the phrase "immense multitude" shows that many of these Christians held strongly to their beliefs and were willing to die rather than recant. Something must be given to explain this kind of spread of a religion based on someone executed as a common criminal. Followers would say it was the resurrection, but critics must find some way to account for this. And any explanation given by them would fall short.[51]

There are hundreds of surviving letters from Pliny the younger, a Roman lawyer from AD 61 to 122. These are an invaluable historical source for the period. Many are addressed to reigning emperors or to other notable figures such as the historian Tacitus. In one such letter he writes to the emperor Trajan for advice on whether he should kill all Christians or just certain ones.

*"I have asked them if they are Christians ... warning of the punishment awaiting them. If they persist, I order them to be led away for execution.... They affirmed, however, that the whole of their guilt, or their error, was that they were in the habit of meeting on a certain fixed day before it was light, when they sang in alternate verse a hymn to Christ as to a god, and bound themselves to a solemn oath, not to do any wicked deeds....*

*This made me decide it was all the more necessary to extract the truth by torture from two slave-women, whom they called deaconesses."*[52]

This was written in AD 111 attesting to the rapid spread of Christianity. It confirms that Christians believed in Jesus as God, met one day a week to worship him, maintained high ethical standards, and were not easily swayed from their beliefs. It also shows us that this belief persisted among slaves and women.[53]

Lucian of Samosata, a Greek satirist from the second century AD, alludes to Christ in his writings.

*"The Christians, you know, worship a man to this day—the distinguished personage who introduced their novel rites, and was crucified on that account.... You see, these misguided creatures start with the general conviction that they are immortal for all time, which explains the contempt of death and voluntary self-devotion which are so common among them; and then it was impressed on them by their original lawgiver that they are all brothers, from the moment that they are converted, and deny the gods of Greece, and worship the crucified sage, and live after his laws. All this they take quite on faith, with the result that they despise all worldly goods alike, regarding them merely as common property."*[54]

This confirms that Christians worshiped a man who was crucified, that they believed in an everlasting spirit, that there is a brotherhood of believers, that they renounced the pagan gods, and that they followed the words and life of Jesus, valuing their faith over their property.

Suetonius, a court official under the emperor Hadrian and Roman historian, confirmed the Gospel claims in several of his works.

In his *Life of Claudius* (written about AD 120), he writes that Christians were expelled from Rome because of Christ (whom he calls Chrestus):

*"As the Jews were making constant disturbances at the instigation of Chrestus, he [Claudius] expelled them from Rome."*[55]

In a separate work, Suetonius records the punishment that Christians were receiving in Rome during the time of Nero (AD 64):

"Punishment by Nero was inflicted on the Christians, a class of men given to a new and mischievous superstition."[56] This "superstition" undoubtedly refers to the conviction by early Christians that Christ had been crucified and risen from the dead.

Other writers in ancient documents referring to Christ include: Epictetus, Aristides, Galenus, Lampridius, DioCassius, Hinnerius, Libanius, Ammianus, Marcellinus, Eunapius, Zosimus, Jewish Talmud (commentary to Jewish law completed in AD 500), and Thallus (AD 52 Samaritan historian).[57]

One expert documented thirty-nine ancient sources that corroborate more than one hundred facts concerning Jesus' life, teachings, crucifixion, and resurrection. Both secular sources and early Christian creeds declare the deity of Jesus was established doctrine in the early church.[58]

From the ancient external sources alone, we can conclude several traits about Jesus and the early Christians.[59]

1. Jesus was a provocative teacher, a wise and virtuous man from the region of Judea
2. Jesus reportedly performed miracles and made prophetic claims
3. The Jewish leaders condemned Him for acts of sorcery and apostasy
4. He was crucified by the Roman procurator Pontius Pilate at the time of the Jewish Passover and during the reign of the Emperor Tiberius
5. Jesus' followers, called Christians, reported that He had risen from the dead
6. The Christian faith had spread to Rome, where Christians were charged with crimes and met horrific persecution
7. First-century Christians worshiped Jesus Christ as God
8. While at times the Romans ridiculed the followers of Christ as morally weak, these Christians were often known for their courage and virtue.

Conclusion

We have to judge this document in the same way that we judge any other piece of historical literature. By those standards we can conclude that the Bible is trustworthy and historically reliable in its witness about Jesus. By assessing the Bible the same way other historical documents are assessed, we find the Bible to be superior in all respects. The manuscript evidence and reliability of the copies we have found through archeology far outweigh any other document from antiquity that is accepted. We can be assured of the credibility of the authors because of the short time span between the events and their writings. The events recorded were even written while other eyewitnesses and critics were still alive. And there are numerous sources outside of the Bible that confirm the New Testament accounts concerning the life, death, and resurrection of Jesus.

> *Scholar F.F. Bruce, in The Books and the Parchments sums it up well: "There is no body of ancient literature in the world which enjoys such a wealth of good textual attestation as the New Testament."*[60]

> *And Dr. Clark H. Pinnock, a professor of systematic theology, states further: "There exists no document from the ancient world witnessed by so excellent a set of textual and historical testimonies, and offering so superb an array of historical data on which an intelligent decision may be made. An honest [person] cannot dismiss a source of this kind. Skepticism regarding the historical credentials of Christianity is based upon an irrational bias."*[61]

## QUESTIONS FOR CONSIDERATION

Why is it necessary to establish the authenticity of Scripture?

How does the manuscript evidence of the New Testament compare to other historical documents?

Why is it important to establish when the New Testament was written?

How can we be confident in the trustworthiness of what was written in the Gospels?

What characteristics of the New Testament authors confirm their credibility? Why does that matter?

How do other works written in the first century affirm the authenticity of the New Testament?

If we consider other works from antiquity to be reliable, shouldn't we consider the New Testament to be reliable as well?

# LESSON 6

## Validity of Jesus Christ

### INTRODUCTION

This is the last lesson of our six-part series. This lesson is where we have been headed since the beginning. We spent three lessons establishing in multiple ways that we can have confidence that a God exists. We know from physics, biology, morality, and logic that an atheist mindset does not sufficiently explain the world we have. There must be something that created and designed it. Since there is a God to whom we owe this existence, it is prudent to determine which God it is. The world has many different types of gods to offer, but all those different religions cannot all be right. We therefore have to search for truth. Christianity sets itself apart as the only religion that effectively addresses our sin nature, our problem of always violating the Moral Law that this God has imparted to us. We know we should behave in a certain way, and we know that we rarely do. Only Christianity provides a solution for us. All other religions provide rules, but none of them provide us righteousness.

The righteousness that Christianity provides is found through Jesus Christ, and the truth about Jesus is found in the New Testament. So we had to establish that the New Testament gives us factual, reliable information about Jesus. The manuscript evidence, credibility of the authors, and confirmation from sources outside the Bible all verify that the New Testament is reliable and truthful. Now that we know that we can trust the Bible as historically accurate, we need to take a look at the main character—Jesus.

**STUDY**

Confidence in the Deity of Christ

*What makes Jesus different?* Everyone is comfortable discussing religion, God, Mohammed, Buddha, and Confucius, but discussing Jesus suddenly makes people upset. Why is that? What sets him apart from other religious leaders?

Jesus claimed something the rest of them did not—He claimed to BE God, not just be a messenger, a preacher, or a teacher of God.[1] *How do we know that was His intent?* Well, the New Testament makes this assertion in three ways:

1. Jesus had characteristics that are characteristics only God can have[2]
   - Self-existent: **John 1:4** (In Him was life); **John 14:6** (I am the way, the truth, and the life)
   - Omnipresent: **Matthew 28:20** (I am with you always); **Matthew 18:20** (where two or more gather, I am there)
   - Omniscient: **John 4:16–20** (woman at the well with multiple husbands); **John 6:64** (for Jesus knew all along who would betray him); **Matthew 17:22–27**

(predicts his death, and asks Peter to get the coin out of the fish's mouth)

- Omnipotent: **Luke 4:38–41** (healed many and cast out demons); **Luke 7:14–15** (raised young child from the dead); **Matthew 8:26–27** (calmed the storm)
- Possesses Eternal Life: **1 John 5:11–12, 20** (whoever has the Son has eternal life); **John 1:4** (in Him is life)
- Receives Godly worship and praise: **Matthew 4:10** (worship the Lord God only); **Matthew 14:33** (those in the boat worshiped Him after He walked on water); **John 5:23** (whoever honors the Son honors the Father); **Hebrews 1:6** (all angels worship the Son); **Revelation 5:8–14** (all will worship the Lamb who was slain and raised)

2. Confessions of those around Him[3]

- This is especially significant considering that His followers were devout Jews who believed in only one true God, yet they confessed Jesus to be God
- Peter—Matthew 16:16–17 (said, "You are the Christ the son of the living God.")
- Martha—John 11:27 (after Lazarus had died says, "I believe that you are the Christ, the Son of God, who is to come into the world.")
- Nathanael—John 1:49 ("Rabbi, you are the Son of God! You are the King of Israel!")
- Stephen—Acts 7:59 (prayed "Lord Jesus receive my spirit" as he was being stoned)
- John the Baptist—John 1:29–34 ("Behold! The Lamb of God who takes away the sin of the world!" at Jesus' baptism; John said, "I have seen and testified that this is the Son of God.")
- Thomas—John 20:26–29 (after doubting the resurrection, "My Lord and my God")

3. Confessions of Jesus Himself

- This is an important point to understand. Some critics say that the disciples misunderstood Jesus and that He never intended to be worshiped as God. Or they claim that we misunderstand that point today. The argument is that Jesus only intended to be a good teacher, but we in our zeal have turned Him into a God. We can show that is not the case if Jesus made those claims Himself.[4]

- John 5:16–18. The Jewish leaders confronted Jesus for healing a man on the Sabbath because that violated the law of resting on the Sabbath. Jesus' response was "**My Father has been working until now, and I have been working**." He referred to God as His own personal Father, not as "our" Father. He put His work on par with God's work, making Him equal to God. The Jewish leaders clearly understood Jesus was claiming to be God. It says they "sought all the more to kill him because He not only broke the Sabbath, but also said that God was His Father, making Himself equal with God."[5]

- In John 10, Jesus was approached by the Jewish leaders who questioned Him about being the Christ. His response was that "I and My Father are one" (verse 30). At this, the Jews picked up stones to stone Jesus. Jesus asks them for which miracle are they stoning him and they replied, "For a good work we do not stone You, but for **blasphemy**, and because You, being a Man, **make Yourself God**." They wanted to stone Jesus because the punishment for blasphemy was stoning (ref. Leviticus 24:16). The Jewish leaders understood exactly what Jesus was claiming, and they were ready to execute Jesus for that claim.[6]

- Jesus looked at Himself as being equal with God by other statements He made:[7]
  - John 8:19 "If you had known Me, you would have known My Father also."
  - John 12:45 "And he who sees Me sees Him who sent Me."
  - John 15:23 "He who hates Me hates My Father also."
  - John 5:23 "All should honor the Son just as they honor the Father. He who does not honor the Son does not honor the Father who sent Him."

- In Mark 2:5 (keeping in mind Mark is the earliest Gospel written), after seeing the demonstration of the paralytic's faith, Jesus forgives the man's sins. The scribes ask by what authority He is able to forgive sins. Jesus responds by asking them which is harder to do—say your sins are forgiven or say arise and walk? And Jesus proceeds to heal the paralytic to show that he has authority to do both.[8]
  - While showing He has the power to heal is more impressive to the eye, His statement about forgiving the man's sins is actually more revealing about His deity. It might appear that anyone can say "You're forgiven," so what can that really prove? Well, you can only say "You're forgiven" if you are the one whom the sins were committed against.
  - If you steal my money I can forgive you. But I can't announce that I forgive you for stealing someone else's money. This man's sins were

against God, so the only one who can forgive those sins is God Himself. Therefore when Jesus said that He could forgive sin, He was staking His claim as God.

- He was forgiving sins as though He was the main person offended by those sins. This only makes sense if He really was the God whose laws are broken and whose love is wounded in every sin.[9]

■ The most definitive evidence of Jesus's claim as God is in His trial. Look in Mark 14:60–64. After Jesus had remained silent before His accusers, the high priest directly asks Jesus "Are you the Christ, the Son of the Blessed?" And Jesus answered, "I am." This is exactly the statement that the Sanhedrin was waiting for. Jesus admitted that He believed He was God, which only could result in two conclusions: He was indeed God or his statement was blasphemy.[10]

- How unusual that this criminal trial was not for what someone had done but for whom someone claimed to be. He was tried and convicted for this claim and this claim alone— blasphemy. So there is no mistaking that Jesus knew the full weight of His claim and He left no question about it for his accusers.

We have proven now by several ways that Jesus indeed claimed to be God and that there was no mistaking that fact. So now we have to decide what to believe about that claim. This was the critical question to answer according to Jesus, as He asked His disciples in Luke 9:18–20, "Who do the crowds say that I am?"

*So who do people say that He is? How does the world usually describe Jesus?* Even those who don't believe Jesus is the Son of God will still typically describe Him in a favorable light. They tend to use words centered on His goodness. They describe Him as a good man, morally upright, a rabbi, a profound teacher, or even a prophet. But this tends to overlook the more radical statements He made about being God. It is that claim that we must assess, because that is what sets Him apart from other religious leaders.

There are three possibilities to a claim such as this one.[11]

1. Jesus wasn't God and knew He wasn't God
2. Jesus wasn't God but thought He really was
3. Jesus was God

Let's look at the evidence of each of those three conclusions to answer the most important question in the Bible, "Who do *you* say that I am?"

## Jesus Wasn't God and Knew He Wasn't

The first scenario is that **Jesus was not God and he knew it;** that makes Jesus a liar. If Jesus made these claims and knew that they were not true, then he was deliberately **lying** and deceiving those who followed him. But if Jesus were lying, then he was also the biggest fool. It was this lie about being God that led to His death. There are other attributes Jesus would have if He were lying about being God.[12]

- He would be a **hypocrite**. One of the most fundamental truths Jesus preached to His disciples was honesty, yet He was living the greatest lie of all time.
- He would be a **false prophet**. He was telling others to trust in Him for their eternal spiritual destiny. Yet He would have known all along that He wasn't God and could do nothing for someone's eternal destiny. He was knowingly convincing people to trust in something that wasn't true.

-  Lying to people so they are eternally damned would make Him **unspeakably evil**.

But evil does not coincide with the teachings or the life of Jesus. He taught kindness and love and promoted morality and honesty. He was Himself morally pure. It would be impossible for Him to consistently maintain the purest and noblest character in all of history while committing the most outrageous deception known to man. He even sacrificed His life to maintain that deception. Those attributes don't stand up with the moral purity and dignity of the life of Jesus that is revealed in every word He spoke and work He did.[13]

Even in His trial, neither the Romans nor the Jewish leaders could find any fault with Him. It was only for His claim of deity that He was convicted, not any deed or sin that he had committed. The Sanhedrin went to great lengths, even promoting perjury, to get testimony from anyone to convict Him. Yet no one could come forward with any sinful act that Jesus had done. It might have been difficult for His enemies to find a sinful act since they were only around Him during His public ministry, a time when someone could be on their best behavior, but even His friends who weren't believers could not find a punishable act committed by Jesus. Those who are closest to us actually know the worst about us. They see us in those moments when we aren't on our best behavior. Your best friend and spouse could find more sin in your life than your worst enemy because your best friend and spouse see you when your guard is let down. So, in His trial, neither friend nor foe could find reason for conviction.

We see this evidence of a life of purity in John 10:32 when Jesus was confronted by the Pharisees. The apostle records, "Then the Jews took up stones again to stone Him. Jesus answered them, 'Many good works I have shown you from My Father. For which of those works do you stone Me?' The Jews answered Him, saying,

'For a good work we do not stone You, but for blasphemy, and because You, being a Man, make Yourself God.'" Even in their anger and attempts to trap Jesus, they still couldn't stone Him for any deed He had done. It still came back to simply who He claimed to be.

We also have to consider the circumstances around this great lie. He chose to come to the Jewish nation where the people so thoroughly adhere to the undivided unity of God. Why not go into Egypt or to Greece or to Rome where they have hundreds of gods in all kinds of manifestations? He certainly wouldn't have needed to sacrifice His life in order to maintain this kind of lie in a place other than Jerusalem. And this is what separates Jesus from other religious founders. Jesus didn't just claim to be *a* god, like the Pharaohs did, he claimed to be *the* God, the one and only true God.[14]

If it were true that He was not God and He knew He wasn't, then we could never describe Him as a good man or morally upright. Because His life was one of purity and of the highest moral standard, we can conclude that Jesus was not evil. Therefore it could not be the case that He wasn't God and knew He wasn't.

*Jesus Wasn't God but Thought He Was*

The second option is that **Jesus was not God**, but He truly **thought He was**. This would make Him crazy. But everything we know about the life of Jesus does not indicate anything a delusional person would say or do.[15] Jesus is known to have spoken some of the most profound statements ever recorded in history. The description of Jesus as a good rabbi or profound moral teacher are a testament to that. Those statements confess that His teachings have sound logic and are coherent, not from a deluded mind.

*Philip Schaff says, "Self-deception in a matter so momentous, and with an intellect in all respects so clear and so sound is equally out of the question. How could he be an enthusiast or a madman who never lost the even balance of his mind, who sailed serenely over all the troubles and persecutions, as the sun above the clouds, who always returned the wisest answer to tempting questions, who calmly and deliberately predicted his death on the cross, his resurrection on the third day, the outpouring of the Holy Spirit, the founding of his church, the destruction of Jerusalem—predictions which have been literally fulfilled?"[16]*

In his book *Miracles*, C.S. Lewis writes:

*"The discrepancy between the depth and sanity ... of His moral teaching and the rampant megalomania which must lie behind His theological teaching unless He is indeed God has never been satisfactorily explained. Hence the non-Christian hypotheses succeed one another with the restless fertility of bewilderment."[17]*

Jesus always exhibits poise and clarity in his statements to his disciples and especially in his responses to the Pharisees' questions. The Pharisees were constantly looking for ways to entrap Jesus. They would have seized on any evidence that Jesus was delusional. But obviously there was nothing Jesus did in his behavior or conversation that gave the slightest indication that he was crazy. If he were just a lunatic, the Pharisees and the Sadducees would not have taken so much time and effort to get rid of Him. They felt truly threatened by Jesus because they knew He was lucid. The Pharisees took Him too seriously for Him to have exhibited any delusional behavior. His delusions would have come out in other ways until the Pharisees would have largely ignored Him.

The Pharisees actually admit to this in Acts 5. Gamaliel, a well-respected Pharisee, points out that other people had come before Jesus and claimed to be the Messiah. But those false prophets faded away because it was not true. The Pharisees would execute the blasphemer and the disciples would scatter. So according to Gamaliel, if Jesus is just some crazy loon like those others, then his disciples would soon scatter and the whole thing will dissipate. But if Jesus really is what He claimed to be, then who are they to fight against God? We have the advantage of knowing what happened to the disciples. The Pharisees executed Jesus, who claimed to be the Messiah, but the disciples did not scatter and dissipate. Quite the contrary. They spread this Gospel of Jesus around the world in the face of intense persecution, even unto death. This confirms Gamaliel's point. Jesus is not just some crazy lunatic, but Jesus really is from God.

If it were true that He was not God and He didn't know it, then we could never describe Him as a good rabbi, a profound teacher, or a prophet. Because His statements were profound and lucid, we can conclude that Jesus was not delusional. Therefore, it could not be the case that He wasn't God but thought He was.

### Jesus Was God

We've shown it is not plausible that Jesus was not God and knew it (liar). And it is not plausible that Jesus was not God and didn't know it (lunatic). His life and teachings do not reflect either of those circumstances. That leaves us with no other option than He is in fact what He claimed to be: God.

Jesus cannot be just a good teacher, a prophet, or an upright religious leader as many people want to classify him. If He is not the first two options, then He must be the third. It is the most probable explanation to who Jesus really is.

You can't make a statement like "I'm God" and it not be true and be considered a good man or a great moral teacher. Because a good and moral man could not claim to be God if it were not true. We do not have the option of simply saying, "He wasn't God, but maybe He was a good man." You can't separate what he taught (good and moral instruction) from who He claimed to be. And He never intended for us to.

As summarized so perfectly by C.S. Lewis:

*"Therefore, we can call him a fool, or we can spit at Him and kill Him as a demon, or we can fall at His feet and call Him Lord and God. But we cannot go with such nonsense as he was just a great teacher. He did not leave that option open to us and He never intended to."*[18]

The apostle John summed up the whole point of his Gospel on this very issue. John 20:31, "But these are written that you may believe that Jesus is the Christ, the **Son of God,** and that believing you may have life in His name."

Confidence in the Resurrection

It is clear that Jesus claimed to be God, and logically that had to be so. But the confirmation of that assertion is also found in the reality of the Resurrection. And belief in the Resurrection is a crucial point to Christianity. Without it, our faith is based on nothing. As Paul says in 1 Corinthians 15:15–19, we should be the most pitied if there is no resurrection from the dead. Jesus' resurrection proves His deity and His power over death. Only by conquering death and sin are we even able to receive salvation. Therefore, it is critical to the foundation of our faith that we have confidence in the resurrection of Jesus. And that is why so many try to discredit the resurrection of Jesus. There are many theories people use to claim that Jesus did not really resurrect from the dead. But upon closer inspection, we can see that these theories are futile attempts at renouncing the truth.

*Resurrection Theories*

Theory: The women who first discovered Jesus' empty tomb went to the wrong tomb.[19]

- Peter and John went to see the tomb for themselves after the women declared it was empty (John 20:3). If the women had gone to the wrong tomb, then Peter and John would have had to go to the wrong tomb as well. It is highly unlikely that all of them visited the wrong tomb.
- Furthermore, the tomb would have been easy to identify since it had soldiers posted on guard and had been sealed with a boulder (Matt. 27:22). Given that the Pharisees were adamant about preventing the disciples from spreading the rumor of his resurrection (which was the point of posting the guards), they would have made sure the guards were standing in front of the right tomb.
- In addition, if the disciples had gone to the wrong tomb and started the rumor that it was empty, the Jewish and Roman authorities would have wasted no time in going to the correct tomb and showing everyone the body of Jesus.

Theory: Jesus simply swooned or fainted on the cross and didn't actually die.[20]

- First, this is an insult to the Romans. The Romans were experts on killing people. They did this for fun and entertainment. Their efficiency at killing was the power behind the vast expansion of the Roman Empire.
- Second, we have the medical evidence from the Roman soldier piercing Jesus' side. When His side was pierced, both water and blood flowed out (John 19:34). The water was a result of the pericardial and pleural effusion (water around the heart and water on the lungs) that are an

indication of hypovolemic shock resulting in heart failure. It is the medical confirmation that Jesus was dead.

- Third, if Jesus had simply passed out, we still have to explain how someone that had been flogged, had thorns shoved into his head, had nails hammered through his hands and feet, and had a spear pierced into His side could roll away the stone from *inside* the tomb. Keep in mind that Jesus had already required assistance in carrying the cross up to Golgotha. So we know that the beating He endured was not something trivial. It is unlikely that being hung on the cross after that would have improved his physical state of being. If after all that Jesus could have opened the tomb from the inside, his appearance to the disciples would not be one of a conqueror of death and the grave (which was the key to their future ministry), but of one that was in dire need of medical attention. That kind of physical appearance would not have changed the disciples from sadness to rejoicing.

Theory: The disciples stole the body.[21]

- The disciples at the time of Jesus' trial were all hiding and denying their association with Jesus out of fear of being arrested too. After the crucifixion, they were in mourning from watching what appeared to be the destruction of their long-awaited Messiah. They were hiding because of their fear of the Jewish authorities. They were not in the mindset to face the danger of killing the Roman guards, risking punishment by death by breaking the Roman seal on the tomb, and stealing the body. Peter denied even knowing Jesus at His trial, so it is improbable to think that after Jesus died on the cross that he would have the gumption to steal the body.

- In reality, the disciples weren't even expecting a resurrection. When the women first told the disciples the tomb was empty, they responded with disbelief, not confidence. Someone who is not expecting a resurrection is unlikely to risk their life to stage a resurrection. In fact, in John's account, the women simply claimed that someone had taken the body. They did not even realize at that moment that Jesus had resurrected.

Theory: The Resurrection was just a legend.[22]

- This was a popular theory among critics who declared the Gospels were written hundreds of years after the time of Christ. The advancements in archeology have proven that is not so. We have affirmed that the Gospel writers were eyewitnesses to those events and had written down their accounts within at most thirty years after the death and resurrection of Jesus. The short time frame and credibility of the authors rule out the theory that the resurrection was just a legend.
- Even the external historical documents from that time period indicate that the religion was founded on the idea that Jesus had resurrected. So we have confidence that this was a church creed from the beginning of the church's founding.

Theory: The people who saw Jesus after his Resurrection were only hallucinating or dreaming.[23]

- First, the followers of Christ were not actually expecting to see Him resurrected, even though Jesus had prophesied of this. The apostles were in mourning in the upper room before Jesus appeared. The women who went to the tomb were going to tend to His dead body, not to find Him resurrected. So there was no expectation among these people that Jesus would actually not be just as dead in three days as He was when they pulled him off the cross.

- Second, there is no explanation for how over 500 people in different locations and of different backgrounds could experience the same hallucination.
- Third, if this were a hallucination, someone would easily be able to show the body in the tomb to expose the resurrection as a hoax. The Pharisees would have gone to the tomb to disprove the rumor of a resurrection.

The one consistent thing with each of these alternative explanations is that they either fail to explain the empty tomb, fail to explain the resurrection appearances, or they fail to explain both.

*Changed Behavior*

The next evidence for the validity of Jesus' identity and His resurrection is the drastic change in the disciples' behavior after the resurrection.

The first change was in their reactions to Jesus. They all loved Jesus and were very devoted to Him. After all, they had abandoned their professions and families to follow Him. But they were still uncertain and probably a little ignorant about the true power of Jesus and the impact of what they were witnessing.[24]

- They bickered over who got to sit at His right and left hand (Mark 10:35–38), not realizing that His kingdom was not of this world.
- The disciples ran and hid when Jesus was arrested, tried, and crucified (Mark 14:50).
- They all mourned his death, not expecting a resurrection.

- Peter denied Jesus three times during the trial.
- Thomas wouldn't believe Jesus had really resurrected until he was able to place his hands in his wounds.
- James, the brother of Jesus, was not even a believer during Jesus' ministry.

Yet after the Resurrection we see the apostles empowered to leave their homes and preach this Resurrection in the face of imprisonment, torture, and eventual death.

- They gained a heavenly perspective and understood the eternal kingdom of Jesus.
- Peter was arrested and imprisoned in the Mamertine prison in Rome. He watched his wife be crucified, and then he was crucified upside down.
- James, brother of Jesus, founded the church in Jerusalem.
- Thomas went outside the Roman Empire to preach the gospel in the Persian Empire and India.
- Throughout the book of Acts, the apostles continued to testify that Jesus was the Son of God and that He resurrected from the dead, even though they were beaten and arrested for that claim.

This change is apparent not only in their statements and actions but in the way they all died. Eleven of the apostles died as martyrs, and all for the same reason: their belief in the Resurrection and their belief that Jesus was the Son of God. They were tortured, flogged, and killed, and all they had to do to save themselves was deny that those two things were true.[25]

- Peter – Crucified (upside down)
- Andrew – Crucified
- Matthew – Killed by sword

- John – Natural death in exile
- James, son of Alphaeus – Crucified
- Philip – Crucified
- Simon – Crucified
- Thaddaeus – Killed by arrows
- James, brother of Jesus – Stoned
- Bartholomew – Crucified
- James, son of Zebedee – Killed by sword
- Thomas – Stoned and stabbed to death
- Stephen – Stoned

We can't discuss the drastic change in the apostles' lives and not address the change in Paul. To summarize his transformation, Saul of Tarsus was excelling in his studies as a Pharisee under the great Gamaliel. He was considered a "Pharisee of Pharisees." Therefore, he hated these followers of Christ because they were in direct opposition to Jewish tradition and Pharisaical law. Saul had already participated in the stoning of the first church martyr, Stephen. And now he was traveling to Damascus with documents giving him authority to seize other followers of Jesus in order to bring them back for trial. It was there that he came face to face with the resurrected Jesus. He was blinded for three days, but in his darkness he understood the truth of who Jesus was. From his conversion experience on that roadside, there were several things to note about the change in Saul—besides his name as Paul.

- Saul's conversion was sincere because <u>he was accepted by the other apostles</u>.[26] When the Lord first spoke to Ananias to go to Saul to restore his sight, Ananias was afraid to go. Saul's reputation was one of persecuting Christians, and now Ananias was told to go speak about Jesus to him. But after his conversion, Saul received the "right hand of fellowship" from the other disciples. He stayed with other disciples for several days there in Damascus (Acts 9:19) preaching boldly in the name of Christ. It was there that his life was already threatened because of his new association with the Christians and he had to flee to Jerusalem. The disciples there were still afraid of him until Barnabas explained Saul's transformation. From that point forward he was welcomed among the disciples as he continued to preach boldly for Christ already in the face of persecution. He was even an important part in the Jerusalem council (Acts 15), along with the other disciples, to settle early doctrinal disputes.

- His message had been transformed.[27] The vision did not simply silence him as a persecutor of Christians. The statement from Jesus on the Damascus road was, "Why do you persecute me?" So one could see that the experience could have just made Saul afraid to continue in the persecution of Christians. But Saul didn't just stop persecuting. He did a complete turnaround to become one of the most outspoken preachers in *favor* of Christianity. He didn't just quit being against Jesus, but he became an ardent follower of Jesus. He went from being the persecutor to being the persecuted, all because of the name of Jesus.

2 Corinthians 11:25–28 *"Three times I was beaten with rods; once I was stoned; three times I was shipwrecked; a night and a day I have been in the deep; in journeys often, in perils of waters, in perils of robbers, in perils of my own countrymen, in perils of the Gentiles, in perils in the city, in perils in the wilderness,*

*in perils in the sea, in perils among false brethren; in weariness and toil, in sleeplessness often, in hunger and thirst, in fastings often, in cold and nakedness— besides the other things, what comes upon me daily: my deep concern for all the churches."*

Therefore, the message he received on the roadside was convincing enough for him to completely change sides. His convictions had changed completely. His experience made him acknowledge that Jesus was the Messiah, which went against all of his training as a Pharisee and the Jewish tradition that he was so adamant to uphold. It went against his current profession and current circle of friends and family. It had to have been a very profound experience for him to turn his back on all of that.

- His mission had changed.[28] Paul went from being a Gentile-hater (as any good Jew at the time would be) to a missionary to the Gentiles. From his upbringing as a Pharisaical Jew, he viewed Gentiles as inferior to the chosen people of God. But after his conversion, Paul's entire mission was to reach the Gentiles and minister to them. In every city, Paul preached first to the Jews in the synagogue and then to the Gentiles in the marketplace.

Lord Lyttleton, an atheist who set out to disprove Saul's conversion concluded, "The conversion and apostleship of Paul alone was of itself a demonstration sufficient to prove Christianity to be a Divine Revelation."[29] He added that if Paul's twenty-five years of suffering and service for Christ were a reality, then his conversion was true, for everything he did in those twenty-five years began from that conversion. And if that conversion were true, then Jesus Christ rose from the dead, for everything Paul became and did, he attributed to the sight of the risen Christ.

What made them change so suddenly? They went from hiding in fear to boldly dying, all for the same claim that Jesus was resurrected. Were they suddenly emboldened by a conspiracy to lie? Only the truth of the resurrection that they witnessed could turn them from heartbroken followers of a crucified rabbi into courageous witnesses and martyrs of the early church. Could they have really turned the world upside down if this was all a lie?

*Would anyone ever die for a lie?* Yes, lots of people have died for a lie.

- *Heaven's Gate cult.* On March 19, 1997, Marshall Applewhite was the leader of the Heaven's Gate group and claimed that a spacecraft was trailing the comet Hale-Bop. He convinced thirty-eight followers to commit suicide so that their souls could board the supposed craft. Applewhite believed that after their deaths, a UFO would take their souls to another "level of existence above human," which Applewhite described as being both physical and spiritual.[30]

- *People's Temple cult.* A communist community in the 70s led by Jim Jones who convinced his 909-member community known as "Jonestown" to all drink Flavor Aid laced with cyanide. The "revolutionary suicide" was supposedly because the Soviet Union would not allow the town members to find refuge there after they murdered five people, including a congressman.[31]

- *September 11, 2001.* Muslim jihadists hijacked planes and flew them into buildings symbolizing American strength and military power. They sacrificed their lives to murder thousands of innocent people in order to earn their spot in the afterlife.

These are all examples of people who willingly died for a lie. Are they any different from the apostles dying for their claims? These examples were those who died for something that they *thought* was the truth. And here's the difference for the apostles: if they knew for a fact that Jesus was not the Son of God and they stole and hid His body to falsify the Resurrection, then they *knew* it was a lie. It is hard enough to die for what is the truth, but people don't die for something that they know is a lie.

If the resurrection were a conspiracy generated by the apostles, at some point under that intense persecution, one of them would have recanted and confessed that it was a hoax. All it would have taken was just one apostle to falter to expose it for a lie, just one of them to face their execution and say, "Okay, we were just making it up. It was all a lie and we hid the body." But that never happened.

The apostles were imprisoned, beaten, and killed, but they could not be made to deny their conviction that Jesus rose from the dead on the third day. And not one single apostle buckled under this immense persecution. These men went from a little band of defeated cowards mourning in an upper room to a powerful, preaching force that no persecution could silence or alter, and did so while adhering to their message of the highest ethical standard the world has ever known. It's absurd to contribute that kind of dramatic change to nothing more than a fabricated story that they were trying to force on the world.

Logically, Jesus must have been what He claimed to be. He must be the Son of God. He proved that with His life and most importantly, with His death and resurrection. After all, that was the whole point of Him leaving His throne room to come down to earth. The evidence from the eyewitness testimony and the obvious impact of the resurrection on those witnesses prove to us that Jesus really is the Son of God and truly resurrected from the grave to pay the penalty that was due to us.

Conclusion

This has been a short journey through some major theological points. It started with trying to understand that there are certain things in this world that we cannot explain without the existence of God. It is intellectually dishonest to try to account for our beginnings with a materialistic and atheistic mindset. It just simply does not hold up under the scrutiny of logic. We are a finite entity and cannot explain our own causation. Something must have caused us to come into being. We are amazingly complex and intricately designed creatures. We have life-critical features that cannot be attributed to random, chaotic chances. Something must have designed us this way from the beginning. We have a spiritual element to us, in that we all have a mind, a drive, a personality—something beyond our physical matter components. However, we cannot arrive at a spirit if we only start with matter. Something spiritual must have created that in us. We have an overarching sense of a moral code that pervades all societies and times. We know some things just ought not be, but we have no way through material and natural means to explain why that is so. Something moral must have imparted to us a sense of morality and a sense of justice.

This Being that is greater than ourselves, the Cause, the Designer, the Spirit, and the Moral Law Giver, must be understood because it is to this Being that we owe our very existence. This Being is knowable because He reveals Himself in everything around us and within us. It is from within us that we desire for justice and for goodness to prevail. In that way, we can be assured the Being who gave us that morality would be interested in justice and goodness as well. And that defines the predicament of mankind. The Being to whom we owe our existence is good and just. In order to be those things, He must hate evil and injustice. But those are the two traits that permeate throughout all of our actions. Everything we do is tainted with evil, injustice, selfishness, and hate. What are we to do about that? Is there anything we can do?

Thousands of religions have been created to try to rectify that situation, but they only seem to provide a set of rules to follow. And while following the rules may seem helpful for a time, it does nothing to repair the rules that have already been broken. And it does nothing to prevent us from continuing to break those rules. The God revealed in the Bible, however, has provided a different path. He has shown that mankind cannot adhere to enough rules to gain righteousness. His justice, therefore, must always be meted out against man. But in His great love, He provided a way to attain righteousness, but it is not through any work that man could do. It was through His own sacrifice of perfection being punished for the imperfect.

This sacrifice comes to us through the New Testament scriptures, a document written two thousand years ago but has greater manuscript attestation than any other ancient work. It was written by those who witnessed firsthand this gift from God to mankind through Jesus, those who walked with Him, were taught by Him, and were loved by Him. It was documented by those who saw Him arrested, beaten, and executed as though He were a common criminal, all because of the claim that He was God. It was recorded by those that saw His resurrection and defeat of death for the benefit of mankind. They spoke with Him, ate with Him, and walked with Him after He was resurrected from the dead. Their lives were forever changed as an attestation of the truth of the life, death, and resurrection of Jesus. Now that we know that Jesus was truly God and He was resurrected from the grave, we have to answer the second greatest question posed in the Bible. In Matthew 27:20, Pilate asked, "What then shall I do with Jesus who is called Christ?" What will *you* do with Jesus who is called Christ?

## QUESTIONS FOR CONSIDERATION

What unique claim sets Jesus apart from other religious leaders?

How do we know we didn't misunderstand that claim?

How do we logically conclude that Jesus' claim of being God was not false?

Why can we not just call Jesus a good man or prophet if He wasn't God?

What are the two things that alternate resurrection theories fail to explain?

How do we know the claims in the New Testament by the apostles were not a conspiracy?

Would a group of people ever die for something that they know to be a lie?

What evidence in the apostle's lives show that the resurrection was real?

Given the characteristics of Jesus' life and the reality of the resurrection, what should we conclude about Jesus? How should that change our lives?

# PARTING WORDS

Congratulations on making it to the end of this study! It has been an extensive, detailed, and profound journey in understanding the reality of God's existence, the unique aspects of Christianity, and the confidence in the deity of Jesus Christ. I applaud you for taking the time to study these things so that you may learn and grow in your faith.

For the believer, I hope from this study you have gained confidence and reassurance of what you believe. I hope it has reaffirmed the amazing attributes of the God we serve and solidified for you the foundation upon which Christianity is built. God created chemistry, biology, astronomy, geology, and philosophy so we do not need to be afraid to look for God in those disciplines. My desire is that you will continue to study the truths about your faith so that you can always be prepared to give a defense for the hope that you have in Christianity. I trust that this book has provided you with answers for your own questions and for those unbelievers around you. Remember, though, these answers and ideas are not to be viewed as weapons with which to beat on the lost world, but as tools to show them that belief in Jesus is secured in reason and logic as well as faith. At the same time, the unbelievers around you must provide reasons for their beliefs as well. So ask them why they believe what they do and how they reached those conclusions. In answering those questions, they must evaluate the validity of their own worldview and the foundation on which they have placed their faith.

For the unbeliever, I hope at a minimum that this study has given you additional things to consider, but ultimately I hope that it has led you to your own belief in Jesus Christ as your Lord and Savior. Regardless, though, the questions raised throughout this study should be taken seriously. Give them great consideration for how they should truly be answered regardless of your preconceived ideas of God and Christianity. There is an amazing Creator that has wonderfully and fearfully made each and every one of us. Understanding who He is and who we are in relation to Him is the most important thing you could do. There is a God who uniquely designed you and who loved you so much that He stepped down to earth for the sole purpose of suffering and dying for you even while you rejected Him. It is from that great love for us that we find mankind has purpose and that life has meaning. In no other endeavor through earthly pleasures or through other religious pursuits can you find eternal satisfaction like you can in salvation through Jesus Christ. I pray most of all that this study has opened your eyes and your hearts to the truth about the amazing life, death, and resurrection of Jesus—and that He did it all for you.

At the end of this study, we know that God exists and that He is morally good and just. We also know that Jesus was truly God and He was resurrected from the grave. Now we each must decide how that will affect our lives.

What will *you* do with Jesus who is called Christ?

# NOTES

## Lesson 1: The Cosmological Argument

1   Lee Strobel, *Case for Faith* (Grand Rapids, MI: Zondervan, 2000), 33–34.

2   R.C. Sproul, *Not a Chance* (Grand Rapids, MI: Baker, 1994), 169.

3   Bert Thompson and Wayne Jackson, *The Case for the Existence of God* (Apologetics Press, Inc., 1996), 4–5.

4   Bert Thompson and Wayne Jackson, *The Case for the Existence of God* (Apologetics Press, Inc., 1996), 5.

5   Bert Thompson and Wayne Jackson, *The Case for the Existence of God* (Apologetics Press, Inc., 1996), 5–6.

6   Mark Mittelberg, *Questions Christians Hope No One Will Ask* (Colorado Springs, CO: Tyndale, 2010), 6–11.

7   http://en.wikipedia.org/wiki/Laws_of_thermodynamics

8   *Not a Chance*, R.C. Sproul, 1994, p. 179–180.

9   Bert Thompson and Wayne Jackson, *The Case for the Existence of God* (Apologetics Press, Inc., 1996), 11.

10  Bert Thompson and Wayne Jackson, *The Case for the Existence of God* (Apologetics Press, Inc., 1996), 11.

11  R.C. Sproul, *Not a Chance* (Grand Rapids, MI: Baker, 1994), 179–180.

12  Bert Thompson and Wayne Jackson, *The Case for the Existence of God* (Apologetics Press, Inc., 1996), 11–12.

13  Norman Geisler, *Christian Apologetics* (Grand Rapids, MI: Baker, 1976), 247.

Lesson 2: The Teleological Argument

1  Bert Thompson and Wayne Jackson, *The Case for the Existence of God* (Apologetics Press, Inc., 1996), 17–18.

2  Richard Dawkins, *The Blind Watchmaker* (New York: W.W. Norton, 1986), dust jacket.

3  Stephen Jay Gould, *The Panda's Thumb*, (New York: W.W. Norton, 1980), 20–21.

4  George B. Schaller, Hu Jinchu, Pan Wenshi, and Zhu Jing, *The Giant Pandas of Wolong* (Chicago, IL: University of Chicago Press, 1985), 4.

5  "Scientists Finally Discover the Function of the Human Appendix" M.B. David, Political Blindspot, 2015. July 22, 2013. http://politicalblindspot.com/scientists-finally-discover-the-function-of-the-human-appendix/

6  Bert Thompson and Wayne Jackson, *The Case for the Existence of God* (Apologetics Press, Inc., 1996), 53.

7  Douglas Futuyma, *Science on Trial* (New York: Pantheon, 1983), 198.

8  Lee Strobel, *The Case for a Creator* (Grand Rapids, MI: Zondervan, 2004), 81–82.

9  Lee Strobel, *The Case for a Creator* (Grand Rapids, MI: Zondervan, 2004), 138.

10  Lee Strobel, *The Case for a Creator* (Grand Rapids, MI: Zondervan, 2004), 139.

11  Bert Thompson and Wayne Jackson, *The Case for the Existence of God* (Apologetics Press, Inc., 1996), 20–21.

12 Lee Strobel, *The Case for a Creator* (Grand Rapids, MI: Zondervan, 2004), 183–184.

13 Bert Thompson and Wayne Jackson, *The Case for the Existence of God* (Apologetics Press, Inc., 1996), 19–20.

14 Bert Thompson and Wayne Jackson, *The Case for the Existence of God* (Apologetics Press, Inc., 1996), 21.

15 Bert Thompson and Wayne Jackson, *The Case for the Existence of God* (Apologetics Press, Inc., 1996), 20.

16 Richard Dawkins, "The Necessity of Darwinism," *New Scientist*, Vol. 94, April 15, 1982, 130.

17 Bert Thompson and Wayne Jackson, *The Case for the Existence of God* (Apologetics Press, Inc., 1996), 26.

18 E.H. Andrews, *From Nothing to Nature* (Welwyn, Hertfordshire, England: Evangelical Press, 1978), 28–29.

19 Margy Kuntz, "Ghost in Your Genes" NOVA Teachers, PBS. org 2007. October 16, 2007. http://www.pbs.org/wgbh/nova/education/activities/3413_genes.html

20 Lee Strobel, *The Case for a Creator* (Grand Rapids, MI: Zondervan, 2004), 232.

21 Bert Thompson and Wayne Jackson, *The Case for the Existence of God* (Apologetics Press, Inc., 1996), 242.

22 Philip E. Johnson, *Darwin on Trial* (Intervarsity Press, 1993), 110.

23 Philip E. Johnson, *Darwin on Trial* (Intervarsity Press, 1993), 112.

24 Lee Strobel, *The Case for a Creator* (Grand Rapids, MI: Zondervan, 2004), 207–213.

25 "Flagellum base diagram en" by Lady of Hats - self-made References: [1], [2], [3] (main 3), [4], [5] (propeller rotation), PMID 17142059 (bend). Licensed under Public Domain via Wikimedia Commons - https://commons.wikimedia.org/wiki/File:Flagellum_base_diagram_en.svg#/media/File:Flagellum_base_diagram_en.svg

26 Lee Strobel, *The Case for a Creator* (Grand Rapids, MI: Zondervan, 2004), 216–219.

27  Lee Strobel, *The Case for a Creator* (Grand Rapids, MI: Zondervan, 2004), 221–223.

28  Michael Behe, "In Defense of the Irreducibility of the Blood Clotting Cascade: Response to Russell Doolittle, Ken Miller, and Keith Robison" *Discovery Institute*, July 31, 2010.

29  Dept. Biology Penn State, 2004, wikispaces.edu, "DNA Structure" https://wikispaces.psu.edu/download/attachments/38807951/DNA_structure.jpg

30  Amoeba Sisters, www.amoebasisters.com, 2015, "DNA Replication: The Cell's Extreme Team Sport"

31  TOK Resource, http://www.tokresource.org, 2015, "3.4 DNA Replication" http://www.tokresource.org/tok_classes/biobiobio/biomenu/dna_replication/index.htm

32  Charles Darwin, *On the Origin of Species* (London: Murray, 1859), 189.

Lesson 3: The Anthropological Argument

1  Lee Strobel, *The Case for a Creator* (Grand Rapids, MI: Zondervan, 2004), 268.

2  Lee Strobel, *The Case for a Creator* (Grand Rapids, MI: Zondervan, 2004), 266.

3  Lee Strobel, *The Case for a Creator* (Grand Rapids, MI: Zondervan, 2004), 269.

4  Lee Strobel, *The Case for a Creator* (Grand Rapids, MI: Zondervan, 2004), 270.

5  Lee Strobel, *The Case for a Creator* (Grand Rapids, MI: Zondervan, 2004), 270.

6  Lee Strobel, *The Case for a Creator* (Grand Rapids, MI: Zondervan, 2004), 272.

7  Wilder Penfield, "Control of the Mind" Symposium at the University of California Medical Center, San Francisco, 1961,

quoted in Arthur Koestler, *Ghost in the Machine* (London: Hutchinson, 1967), 203.

8   Wilder Penfield, *The Mystery of the Mind*, 77–78.

9   Lee Strobel, *The Case for a Creator* (Grand Rapids, MI: Zondervan, 2004), 273.

10  Lee Strobel, *The Case for a Creator* (Grand Rapids, MI: Zondervan, 2004), 273–274.

11  Lee Strobel, *The Case for a Creator* (Grand Rapids, MI: Zondervan, 2004), 281.

12  Lee Strobel, *The Case for a Creator* (Grand Rapids, MI: Zondervan, 2004), 275.

13  Lee Strobel, *The Case for a Creator* (Grand Rapids, MI: Zondervan, 2004), 278.

14  Lee Strobel, *The Case for a Creator* (Grand Rapids, MI: Zondervan, 2004), 279.

15  Lee Strobel, *The Case for a Creator* (Grand Rapids, MI: Zondervan, 2004), 286.

16  Stuart C. Hackett, *The Reconstruction of the Christian Revelation Claim*, (Grand Rapids, MI: Baker, 1984), 111.

17  John Njoroge, RZIM Academy Course-024, 2015, Lecture 6.1, "God and Morality"

18  C.S. Lewis, *Mere Christianity* (New York, NY: HarperCollins, 1980), 3.

19  C.S. Lewis, *Mere Christianity* (New York, NY: HarperCollins, 1980), 8.

20  C.S. Lewis, *Mere Christianity* (New York, NY: HarperCollins, 1980), 8.

21  C.S. Lewis, *Mere Christianity* (New York, NY: HarperCollins, 1980), 19.

22  C.S. Lewis, *Mere Christianity* (New York, NY: HarperCollins, 1980), 18.

23  C.S. Lewis, *Mere Christianity* (New York, NY: HarperCollins, 1980), 10.

24  C.S. Lewis, *Mere Christianity* (New York, NY: HarperCollins, 1980), 10.

25  C.S. Lewis, *Mere Christianity* (New York, NY: HarperCollins, 1980), 11.

26  C.S. Lewis, *Mere Christianity* (New York, NY: HarperCollins, 1980), 12.

27  C.S. Lewis, *Mere Christianity* (New York, NY: HarperCollins, 1980), 6.

28  Ravi Zacharias, RZIM Academy Course-024, 2015, Lecture 5.1, "Can Man Live without God?"

29  Kai Nielsen, "Why Should I Be Moral?" *American Philosophical Quarterly 21* (1984), 90.

30  John Njoroge, RZIM Academy Course-024, 2015, Lecture 6.1, "God and Morality"

31  John Lennox, *Beyond Opinion: Living the Faith that We Defend* (Nashville: Thomas Nelson, 2008), 113.

32  John Njoroge, RZIM Academy Course-024, 2015, Lecture 6.1, "God and Morality"

33  Richard Rorty quoted in David Berlinski. *The Devil's Delusion, Atheism and its Scientific Pretentions* (New York: Crown Forum, 2008), 40.

34  C.S. Lewis, *Mere Christianity* (New York, NY: HarperCollins, 1980), 13.

35  C.S. Lewis, *Mere Christianity* (New York, NY: HarperCollins, 1980), 13.

36  Mark Twain, *Following the Equator,* Pudd'nhead Wilson's New Calendar (Hartford, CT: American Publishing Company, 1897), Chapter 28 epigraph.

37  Charles Darwin, *The Descent of Man* (Amherst, NY: Promeheus Books, 1998), 102.

38  John Njoroge, RZIM Academy Course-024, 2015, Lecture 6.1, "God and Morality"

39  C.S. Lewis, *Mere Christianity* (New York, NY: HarperCollins, 1980), 30–31.

Lesson 4: Religious Exclusivity

1  "Aren't All Religions Equally Valid?" Andy Bannister, RZIM. org Ravi Zacharias International Ministries, 2015. 1 August 2012. http://rzim.org/a-slice-of-infinity/arent-all-religions-equally-valid

2  R.C. Sproul, *Choosing My Religion* (Phillipsburg, NJ: P&R Publishing Company, 2005), 27.

3  R.C. Sproul, *Choosing My Religion* (Phillipsburg, NJ: P&R Publishing Company, 2005), 11.

4  "Aren't All Religions Equally Valid?" Andy Bannister, RZIM. org Ravi Zacharias International Ministries, 2015. 1 August 2012. http://rzim.org/a-slice-of-infinity/arent-all-religions-equally-valid

5  "Aren't all religions the same? Is Christ the only way to God?" FaithFacts.org Faith Facts, 2008. http://www.faithfacts.org/search-for-truth/questions-of-christians/arent-all-religions-the-same

6  R.C. Sproul, *Choosing My Religion* (Phillipsburg, NJ: P&R Publishing Company, 2005), 16.

7  Ravi Zacharias, *Jesus Among Other Gods* (Nashville, TN: Thomas Nelson, 2000), 6.

8  "Aren't all religions the same? Is Christ the only way to God?" FaithFacts.org Faith Facts, 2008. http://www.faithfacts.org/search-for-truth/questions-of-christians/arent-all-religions-the-same

9  Lee Strobel, *The Case for Faith* (Grand Rapids, MI: Zondervan, 2000), 149.

10  *The Apologetics Study Bible* (Nashville, TNL Holman Bible Publishers, 2007), Appendix: Comparisons of World Religion.

11  Ravi Zacharias, *Jesus Among Other Gods* (Nashville, TN: Thomas Nelson, 2000), 90.

12  "The Spiritual Needs of the Dying: A Buddhist Perspective" Ven. Pende Hawter, Buddha Dharma Education Association, 1996–2012. August 1995. http://www.buddhanet.net/spirit_d.htm

13  Andy Bannister, RZIM Academy Course-024, 2015, Lecture 9.1, "Understanding Islam"

14  Ravi Zacharias, *Jesus Among Other Gods* (Nashville, TN: Thomas Nelson, 2000), 71–72.

15  "Preparing Mind for Meditation" The Foundation of Buddhist Thought, Jamyang Buddhist Centre, London. http://www.buddhistthought.org/study-centre/daily-meditation/preparing-mind-for-meditation/

16  "Preparing Mind for Meditation" The Foundation of Buddhist Thought, Jamyang Buddhist Centre, London. http://www.buddhistthought.org/study-centre/daily-meditation/preparing-mind-for-meditation/

17  "Some questions about Buddhist Prayer / Chanting" New Buddhist. January 2005. http://newbuddhist.com/discussion/91/some-questions-about-buddhist-prayer-chanting

18  "How to Perform Wudhu and Tayammum" http://www.al-islam.org/nutshell/laws_practices/1.htm

19  Ravi Zacharias, *Jesus Among Other Gods* (Nashville, TN: Thomas Nelson, 2000), 162.

20  Ravi Zacharias, *Jesus Among Other Gods* (Nashville, TN: Thomas Nelson, 2000), 89.

21  Ravi Zacharias, *Jesus Among Other Gods* (Nashville, TN: Thomas Nelson, 2000), 73.

22  Ravi Zacharias, *Jesus Among Other Gods* (Nashville, TN: Thomas Nelson, 2000), 90.

23  "Aren't all religions the same? Is Christ the only way to God?" FaithFacts.org Faith Facts, 2008. http://www.faithfacts.org/search-for-truth/questions-of-christians/arent-all-religions-the-same

24  Lee Strobel, *The Case for Faith* (Grand Rapids, MI: Zondervan, 2000), 145.

25  Lee Strobel, *The Case for Faith* (Grand Rapids, MI: Zondervan, 2000), 150.

26  Ravi Zacharias, *Jesus Among Other Gods* (Nashville, TN: Thomas Nelson, 2000), 181.

27  Lee Strobel, *The Case for Faith* (Grand Rapids, MI: Zondervan, 2000), 151 & 153.

28  Lee Strobel, *The Case for Faith* (Grand Rapids, MI: Zondervan, 2000), 163.

29  Lee Strobel, *The Case for Faith* (Grand Rapids, MI: Zondervan, 2000), 162.

Lesson 5: Validity of the New Testament

1  C. Sanders, *Introduction to Research in English Literary History* (New York: MacMillan Company, 1952), 143ff.

2  Lee Strobel, *Case for Christ* (Grand Rapids, MI: Zondervan, 1998), 34.

3  Lee Strobel, *Case for Christ* (Grand Rapids, MI: Zondervan, 1998), 61–62.

4  Lee Strobel, *Case for Christ* (Grand Rapids, MI: Zondervan, 1998), 89.

5  Josh McDowell, *More Than a Carpenter* (Wheaton, IL: Living Books, 1977), 43.

6  Josh McDowell, *More Than a Carpenter* (Wheaton, IL: Living Books, 1977), 43.

7  Kenneth Richard Samples, *Without a Doubt* (Grand Rapids, MI: Baker Books, 2004), 99.

8  Lee Strobel, *Case for Christ* (Grand Rapids, MI: Zondervan, 1998), 34.

9  Lee Strobel, *Case for Christ* (Grand Rapids, MI: Zondervan, 1998), 34.

10  Josh McDowell, *More Than a Carpenter* (Wheaton, IL: Living Books, 1977), 44.

11  Josh McDowell, *Evidence for Christianity* (Nashville, TN: Thomas Nelson, 2006), 79.

12  Lee Strobel, *Case for Christ* (Grand Rapids, MI: Zondervan, 1998), 35.

13  Kenneth Richard Samples, *Without a Doubt* (Grand Rapids, MI: Baker Books, 2004), 93.

14  Kenneth Richard Samples, *Without a Doubt* (Grand Rapids, MI: Baker Books, 2004), 93.

15  Josh McDowell, *More Than a Carpenter* (Wheaton, IL: Living Books, 1977), 47.

16  Josh McDowell, *More Than a Carpenter* (Wheaton, IL: Living Books, 1977), 47.

17  Josh McDowell, *More Than a Carpenter* (Wheaton, IL: Living Books, 1977), 48.

18  Lee Strobel, *Case for Christ* (Grand Rapids, MI: Zondervan, 1998), 60.

19  Lee Strobel, *Case for Christ* (Grand Rapids, MI: Zondervan, 1998), 60.

20  Lee Strobel, *Case for Christ* (Grand Rapids, MI: Zondervan, 1998), 60.

21  Kenneth Richard Samples, *Without a Doubt* (Grand Rapids, MI: Baker Books, 2004), 92.

22  Josh McDowell, *Evidence for Christianity* (Nashville, TN: Thomas Nelson, 2006), 60–61.

23  Josh McDowell, *Evidence for Christianity* (Nashville, TN: Thomas Nelson, 2006), 60–61.

24  Kenneth Richard Samples, *Without a Doubt* (Grand Rapids, MI: Baker Books, 2004), 93.

25  Kenneth Richard Samples, *Without a Doubt* (Grand Rapids, MI: Baker Books, 2004), 94.

26 Kenneth Richard Samples, *Without a Doubt* (Grand Rapids, MI: Baker Books, 2004), 94.

27 Kenneth Richard Samples, *Without a Doubt* (Grand Rapids, MI: Baker Books, 2004), 94.

28 Frederic Kenyon, *The Bible and Archaeology* (NY: Harper, 1940), 288–289.

29 John Warwick Montgomery, *History and Christianity* (Minneapolis, MN: Bethany, 1965).

30 Josh McDowell, *Evidence for Christianity* (Nashville, TN: Thomas Nelson, 2006), 129–130.

31 Millar Burrows, *The Dead Sea Scrolls* (New York: Random House Publishing, 1988), 304.

32 Mark Mittelberg, *Questions Christians Hope No One Will Ask* (Colorado Springs, CO: Tyndale, 2010), 79.

33 Lee Strobel, *Case for Christ* (Grand Rapids, MI: Zondervan, 1998), 66–67.

34 Josh McDowell, *More Than a Carpenter* (Wheaton, IL: Living Books, 1977), 49.

35 Kenneth Richard Samples, *Without a Doubt* (Grand Rapids, MI: Baker Books, 2004), 97–98.

36 Lawrence J. McGinley, *Form Criticism of the Synoptic Healing Narratives* (Woodstock: Woodstock College Press, 1944), 25.

37 Kenneth Richard Samples, *Without a Doubt* (Grand Rapids, MI: Baker Books, 2004), 96.

38 Kenneth Richard Samples, *Without a Doubt* (Grand Rapids, MI: Baker Books, 2004), 97.

39 Kenneth Richard Samples, *Without a Doubt* (Grand Rapids, MI: Baker Books, 2004), 97.

40 Norman Geisler, *Christian Apologetics* (Grand Rapids, MI: Baker Publishing Group, 2013), 350.

41 A.N. Sherwin-White, *Roman Society & Roman Law in the New Testament* (Oxford: Clarendon Press, 1963), 189.

42 Josh McDowell, *More Than a Carpenter* (Wheaton, IL: Living Books, 1977), 54.

43 Lee Strobel, *Case for Christ* (Grand Rapids, MI: Zondervan, 1998), 49.

44 Lee Strobel, *Case for Christ* (Grand Rapids, MI: Zondervan, 1998), 45.

45 Lee Strobel, *Case for Christ* (Grand Rapids, MI: Zondervan, 1998), 48.

46 Eusebius *Ecclesiastical History*, Book 3, Ch. 39.

47 Irenaeus, *Adversus haereses* 3.1.1 & 3.3.4

48 F.F. Bruce, Jesus and Christian Origins Outside the New Testament (Grand Rapids, MI: Eerdans, 1974).

49 Josephus, *Antiquities* 20.9.1 & 18.33

50 Tacitus, *Annals* 15.44

51 Lee Strobel, *Case for Christ* (Grand Rapids, MI: Zondervan, 1998), 82–83.

52 Pliny the Younger, *Letters* 10.96

53 Lee Strobel, *Case for Christ* (Grand Rapids, MI: Zondervan, 1998), 84.

54 Lucian, On the Death of Peregrine 11–13.

55 Suetonius, *Life of Claudius* 25.4

56 Suetonius, Lives of the Caesars 26.2

57 Kenneth Richard Samples, *Without a Doubt* (Grand Rapids, MI: Baker Books, 2004), 95.

58 Lee Strobel, *Case for Faith* (Grand Rapids, MI: Zondervan, 2000), Appendix A, 264.

59 Kenneth Richard Samples, *Without a Doubt* (Grand Rapids, MI: Baker Books, 2004), 95.

60 F.F. Bruce *The Books and the Parchments* (New York: Harper Collins, 1963), 178.

61 Clark Pinnock, *Set Forth Your Case* (New Jersey: The Craig Press, 1968), 58.

Lesson 6: Validity of Jesus Christ

1  Josh McDowell, *More Than a Carpenter* (Wheaton, IL: Living Books, 1977), 10.

2  Josh McDowell, *More Than a Carpenter* (Wheaton, IL: Living Books, 1977), 11–12.

3  Josh McDowell, *More Than a Carpenter* (Wheaton, IL: Living Books, 1977), 12–14.

4  Josh McDowell, *More Than a Carpenter* (Wheaton, IL: Living Books, 1977), 14–16.

5  Josh McDowell, *More Than a Carpenter* (Wheaton, IL: Living Books, 1977), 14–16.

6  Josh McDowell, *More Than a Carpenter* (Wheaton, IL: Living Books, 1977), 16–17.

7  Josh McDowell, *More Than a Carpenter* (Wheaton, IL: Living Books, 1977), 17.

8  Josh McDowell, *More Than a Carpenter* (Wheaton, IL: Living Books, 1977), 18.

9  C.S. Lewis, *Mere Christianity* (New York, NY: HarperCollins, 1980), 51–52.

10 Josh McDowell, *More Than a Carpenter* (Wheaton, IL: Living Books, 1977), 20.

11 Josh McDowell, *More Than a Carpenter* (Wheaton, IL: Living Books, 1977), 27.

12 Josh McDowell, *More Than a Carpenter* (Wheaton, IL: Living Books, 1977), 27–28

13 Philip Schaff, *History of the Christian Church* (Grand Rapids, MI: Eerdmans Publishing Company, 1962), 109.

14 Josh McDowell, *More Than a Carpenter* (Wheaton, IL: Living Books, 1977), 30

15 Josh McDowell, *More Than a Carpenter* (Wheaton, IL: Living Books, 1977), 30–31

16 Philip Schaff, *History of the Christian Church* (Grand Rapids, MI: Eerdmans Publishing Company, 1962), 109.

17 C.S. Lewis, *Miracles: A Preliminary Study* (New York: The MacMillan Company, 1947), 113.

18 C.S. Lewis, *Mere Christianity* (New York, NY: HarperCollins, 1980), 52.

19 Josh McDowell, *More Than a Carpenter* (Wheaton, IL: Living Books, 1977), 93.

20 Lee Strobel, *Case for Christ* (Grand Rapids, MI: Zondervan, 1998), 199, 201–202

21 Josh McDowell, *More Than a Carpenter* (Wheaton, IL: Living Books, 1977), 95.

22 Dr. James Kennedy, *Why I Believe* (Dallas, TX: Word Publishing, 1980), 113.

23 Dr. James Kennedy, *Why I Believe* (Dallas, TX: Word Publishing, 1980), 114.

24 Josh McDowell, *More Than a Carpenter* (Wheaton, IL: Living Books, 1977), 64.

25 Josh McDowell, *More Than a Carpenter* (Wheaton, IL: Living Books, 1977), 61.

26 Josh McDowell, *More Than a Carpenter* (Wheaton, IL: Living Books, 1977), 83.

27 Josh McDowell, *More Than a Carpenter* (Wheaton, IL: Living Books, 1977), 83–84.

28 Josh McDowell, *More Than a Carpenter* (Wheaton, IL: Living Books, 1977), 85.

29 Baron George Lyttleton, Observations on the Conversion and Apostleship of St. Paul: In a Letter to Gilbert West (London: Pall-Mall, 1747), 2.

30 https://en.wikipedia.org/wiki/Heaven%27s_Gate_(religious_group)

31 https://en.wikipedia.org/wiki/Peoples_Temple

# DEFEND THE FAITH MINISTRY

Defend the Faith Ministry works to provide the resources to help individuals and small groups understand why they can have confidence in the Bible and its promises – and how to share that confidence with others. Defend the Faith Ministry is focused on preparing believers to face the battles in a world of skepticism, equipping them to be effective witnesses, and providing them the tools to teach others these truths as well.

For more information about Defend the Faith Ministry, visit: www.defendthefaithministry.com

# ABOUT THE AUTHOR

Cathryn Buse was born and raised in Birmingham, Alabama. She attended the University of Alabama in Huntsville graduating summa cum laude with Bachelor and Master Degrees in Engineering. Cathryn worked for ten years in the engineering field supporting Department of Defense programs, commercial rocket manufacturing, and NASA design programs. From her experience in the technical arena, Cathryn saw that people had deep foundational criticisms about religion and Christianity. Out of her desire to help others see the reason and truth behind the Christian faith, she began studying apologetics on her own as well as through the Ravi Zacharias International Ministry Academy. Recognizing the need for others to have this same foundation, Cathryn began teaching these fundamental truths to others. For nearly a decade, Cathryn has been teaching apologetics to students at her church and to adults of all backgrounds and denominations in her community. Cathryn has since founded the Defend the Faith Ministry to help others learn and share the truth of Christianity.